My Mother's Garden

My Mother's Garden

A Collection about

Love, Flowers, and Family

INTRODUCTION BY PENELOPE HOBHOUSE

CHAMBERLAIN BROS.
A MEMBER OF PENGUIN GROUP (USA) INC.
NEW YORK

CHAMBERLAIN BROS.
Published by the Penguin Group
Penguin Group (USA) Inc., 375 Hudson Street, New York, New York 10014, USA
Penguin Group (Canada), 10 Alcorn Avenue, Toronto, Ontario M4V 3B2, Canada (a division of Pearson Penguin Canada Inc.)
Penguin Books Ltd, 80 Strand, London WC2R 0RL, England
Penguin Ireland, 25 St Stephen's Green, Dublin 2, Ireland (a division of Penguin Books Ltd)
Penguin Group (Australia), 250 Camberwell Road, Camberwell, Victoria 3124, Australia (a division of Pearson Australia Group Pty Ltd)
Penguin Books India Pvt Ltd, 11 Community Centre, Panchsheel Park, New Delhi–110 017, India
Penguin Group (NZ), Cnr Airborne and Rosedale Roads, Albany, Auckland 1310, New Zealand (a division of Pearson New Zealand Ltd)
Penguin Books (South Africa) (Pty) Ltd, 24 Sturdee Avenue, Rosebank, Johannesburg 2196, South Africa

Penguin Books Ltd, Registered Offices: 80 Strand, London WC2R 0RL, England

An application has been submitted to register this book with the Library of Congress.

ISBN 1-59609-147-9

Printed in the United States of America
10 9 8 7 6 5 4 3 2 1

Book design by Jaime Putorti

C O N T E N T S

INTRODUCTION

by Penelope Hobhouse

I do not blame anyone else for a less-than-horticultural childhood; I must have been singularly unresponsive. We lived in Ireland, and in our pre–World War II life—I was nine when war broke out in 1939—there was an old walled garden for fruit and vegetables tended by two stalwart workers. My mother also had a flower garden for cutting for the house. So I was in no sense deprived but remained totally unconnected to the world of plants. I am very envious of those who discovered flowers and gardens at their mother's knee. I do remember drifting through my very ancient grandmother's Edwardian flower garden: gravel paths, rose arbors, scent, and color. What I discovered then was a great joy in its beauty. It also fulfilled my need for a feeling of seclusion, for solitude, and for somewhere to escape from the real world. I like to think that the experience shaped my own design work, in which I try to implement this desire for a refuge, a place apart.

At home, our privileged life came to an end in 1939, and my

first conscious gardening enthusiasm was not awakened until the 1950s when I was married and settled, wanting passionately to make a garden and grow fresh vegetables. Then I was lucky to have distinguished neighbors as generous mentors. Margery Fish, author of countless inspirational books about cottage gardening, lived nearby at East Lambrook in Somerset. She gave me plants and let me absorb some of her wisdom. Sir John and Lady Heathcoat-Amory at Knightshayes, now a famous National Trust garden on a grand scale, took me under their wing and pushed me along the right road toward learning plant names and beginning to have a glimmering sense of design.

This collection of essays, all by people with fond memories of early garden teachers, makes me envious. It is not only the wisdom shared between generations; often the contributors reveal some depth of emotion made more solid by the practical act of tending flowers with a close and loving relation. How enjoyable it would have been to have started sooner, with a childhood experience and magical memories of a beloved teacher. Although I have been lucky since, I am sad to have missed this; it might also have saved me from many mistakes and failures.

So many gardeners I meet seem, literally, to have learned about plants and gardening as they learned to walk. Not only did they absorb the names of flowers but they also summon evocative memories of cherished garden enclosures. Perhaps the most famous of our English garden writers, Christopher Lloyd is a fine example. He credits his mother with his inspiration. Doubly fortunate, he still lives in the family home created, with Edwin Lutyens' help, by his parents. Great Dixter is not only one of the best British gardens today but Christopher must retain dramatic early memories. My neighbor in southwest England is Anna Pavord, famous for her book *The Tulip*. She speaks of her mother's botanical knowledge with affection and awe. Her childhood recollection of a mountainside in Wales has played a part in stimulating her interest in plant *genera* and design.

I have had to research gardening through other people's experience. Celia Thaxter (1835–1894) is not a bad place to start. In *An Island Garden*, written in 1893, the last year of her life, she tells the story of her garden on Appledore, one of the Isles of Shoal, off the coast of Maine. The tale, illustrated evocatively by the impressionist painter Childe Hassam (1859–1935), is still as pure and fresh as when she wrote it. A poet as well as a writer, Thaxter is a practical gardener, battling against salt-ridden gales with a heavy board fence, fighting off predatory birds and slugs, and digging, weeding, watering, planting, and pruning through the summer season. In a space fifty by fifteen feet she grew over fifty different species. She created a garden of great beauty to which she attracted the literary and artistic luminaries of New England. Although she was married with children, there is no record of the children's early participation.

Instead, she wrote about her garden to inspire countless new generations. Her niece, aged only two when Thaxter died, describes keeping the garden going through later years. Thaxter's story is a beloved text for every aspiring gardener. Today, the garden on Appledore has been renewed by a charitable trust.

All gardening is a labor of love and dedication, but creating something beautiful becomes more meaningful when the daily tasks relate nostalgically to childhood memories, which provide an intuitive background to grown-up garden ventures. There is a framework of old absorbed experience. Learning to garden without a familiar background is that much harder. Seasonal rituals of bulb planting, splitting up perennials, mulching, weeding, pruning, deadheading, and cutting flowers for the house were all new to me. For others, each skill brings back thoughts of the past. Sometimes these personal reminders include moments of frustration and failure; even for mothers and grandmothers gardening was not always a bed of roses.

My Mother's Garden: A Collection about Love, Flowers, and Family is full of tender reminiscence. It is also the perfect episodic book for bedside "dipping." It is not about the garden fashions and styles of grand estates. It is about real people and how they enjoyed growing things, and gardened for pleasure and sustenance, often through difficult years when money to be spent on flowers was always tight and depended on seed collection and "sharing" with neighbors.

The book is about much-loved gardens where flowers and vegetables thrived together. Although mainly about "cottage" gardens, it is not about those that became fashionable as a cult during the last hundred years. It is about tradition and informality, gardens tied to their setting, often part of a larger agricultural holding. These were an integrated element of domestic life in which cooking, preserving, and drying were as important tasks as seasonal cultivation and sowing. These gardens were and are part of the vernacular of American garden development. They were not always romantic in intent although memory often lends a romantic aura, as the selective mind trims out the unwanted and perhaps harsher detail.

My Mother's Garden includes writings by an eclectic selection of authors (mainly women), all of whom have become achievers, although not necessarily in the horticultural world. It is sensitive, inspiring, gentle, often joyful, and sometimes sad. Above all, it is full of personal Proustian-type memories in which emotions run deep. Of course, it is not only about mothers; it includes grandmothers, siblings, aunts, and uncles. Sometimes it waxes poetic, but the poetry is always full of garden and flower imagery. Stories include the travels of a treasured seed sack carried west to Oregon by pioneering women in the 1840s much as the seventeenth-century settlers in colonial America brought "slips" (roots and seeds) of old-fashioned favorites from their European countries of origin.

On the banks of the Willamette, Charlotte Kirkwood's mother grew fragrant English sweetbriar roses and delicately scented pinks, spreading the gospel of gardening among her hardworking neighbors and enticing exotic butterflies and hummingbirds from the southern hemisphere. Louise Hallberg carries the story further—to her nonprofit Butterfly Garden in Sebastopol, California, to which visitors flock today to admire the forty different species drawn there by fragrance and nectar. Another story, this time by Linda Frank, not only deals with seed growing but also with a child's love for her mother and a young boy's dedication to creating a flower garden in an urban wasteland mainly populated by seedling stinkweed trees. It tells of initiation into the gardening fraternity.

Quite differently, Jamaica Kincaid manages in her tale "The Garden in Winter" to tell another human story. It points out the unfortunate truth that people bound together by close family ties—in this case, mother and daughter—which they did not choose and cannot help, do not always share a loving relationship. I would like to know more about the lasagna gardening practiced by Patricia Lanza, who was reared by her grandmother, apron- and quilt-maker, chicken farmer and gardener, in eastern Tennessee during the Great Depression. Her childhood, hard and deprived by modern standards, was enriched by their shared experience. Today she is a well-known columnist, broadcaster, and garden writer. It is one of the most touching tales in this collection. And there are many more—too many to mention individually.

Other entries emphasize the importance of garden produce, an insurance against hardship in winter. Apple orchards, peach trees, gooseberries for pies, and black haws from the hedgerows all play a role in looking back to country women who, struggling to make a life, found time to appreciate the magic of a field of daisies: "in a world of constant work, sometimes wonder trumps utility."

As you would expect, scent plays a significant role in nostalgic memories. Children remember people and places through their olfactory senses almost before they can articulate their feelings. It is not only the perfumed air of sweet peas and roses, jasmine and gardenias, and "the scent of peaches drying on a roof," that charm and comfort, wafting back the memories. It is also the smell of compost, of friable earth and woodland vegetation after rain, all of which have a story to tell and a place to expose. Later, as the eye becomes more aware, garden memories are suffused with brilliant color: dahlias, delphiniums, forsythias, petunias, sunflowers, verbena, and zinnias.

In "A River of Sunlight," Grandmother Lovejoy is the inspiration, her garden a haven for flowers, edible plants, and wildlife, brought to us by a piece of brilliant writing. I feel envious of her granddaughter Sharon. A well-known author, Sharon's own gardening books reflect the grandmotherly influence. Birds, totally unfamiliar to me, make short work of a plague of caterpillars. Hummingbirds scold from scarlet bottlebrushes and gold-belted bumblebees search for nectar in blue morning glories. Can it all be true? It seems like perfection. Is this what gardening is meant to be: a secret world "in a river of sunlight and fragrance"? Over all these recollections there is a hovering presence, the benevolent creator of order and beauty whose hard work improves nature's bounty.

One entry must remain my favorite; it is familiar to most of us. In an extract from Frances Hodgson Burnett's *The Secret Garden*, it is Dickon's mother who plays the leading part after her son sings to the children, Mary and Colin, and to the old gardener, Ben Weatherstaff. There is magic in the air as both Colin and Mary, intent on weeding the old hidden garden, change from sickly, cross children at odds with each other into healthy, happy companions. Dickon's mother holds the key to how gardens animate the soul. And the act of gardening has transformed selfish invalids with joyful fulfillment.

Gardens are our own personal sanctuaries, reflecting our need for solitude and stillness, places for meditation and reflection. But they are also able to evoke long forgotten memories. The writers in My *Mother's Garden* pay loving tribute to a past which helped to shape their future.

My Mother's Garden

CHAPTER 1

"Gardening with My Mother"

by Rose Marie Nichols McGee

Gardening can sink its roots deep into a family and so it is with mine. Perhaps this is just another way of saying we come from sturdy European peasant stock with strong gardening traditions. When I was a child, my mother told me stories of her mother's gardening and how her mother, each summer, would plant the path to their house with fragrant Four-o'clocks that opened to greet my grandfather as he returned from work. Every year they had a large vegetable garden that included potatoes. Some of these my mother would dig with her brother and sister and they would then walk out onto the plains outside their hometown of Pueblo, Colorado. There they would build a fire and roast homegrown potatoes. How jealous I was at the thought of this trio of siblings with such freedom they were allowed to spend a harmless carefree day, nourished by sun, air, potatoes, and salt.

My own mother loved to meld the esoteric with the basics. We lived on what can only be called a farmette . . . too small for serious agriculture but sufficient space to grow whatever interested my parents. Mother had a great respect for process and technique. She would read up on the literature and find instructions for each new endeavor and then set to work. My parents were developing a small retail nursery at our home and Mother became interested in growing pansies. She carefully sifted soil and compost through a wire screen to prepare her seedbed, sowed the seeds, and covered them with burlap bags. She explained how it was important to keep them moist all the time until germination and that pansies would sprout best in darkness. Twice a day the bags were sprinkled and my sister and I would peer in at the seeds. In about a week healthy sprouts suddenly emerged and off came the burlap because now the new leaves needed light to photosynthesize and grow. So I learned early on the concept of photosynthesis and the care required to grow new plants. We weren't done yet, and all of us worked together to transplant the seedlings into larger beds. Soon there were more healthy blooming pansies than she could ever use, so a small ad was placed in the paper. After the third customer came out and started pointing to the specific plants they would like dug, only to change their minds a couple of times, she wised up. We transplanted a good selection to small pots so customers could help themselves. Their nursery always had pansy plants and when they developed our seed company, pansy seeds from all over the world were an early specialty.

As soon as they moved onto their property my parents began planting a garden and a carefully selected home orchard. We had several varieties of cherries, plums, apples, and quince along with a selection of berries and unusual shrub fruits. Roses, forsythia, bulbs, camellias, and holly gaily provided seasonal color through most of the year. Some of those garden delicacies were the bane of my childhood summers. Worst were the red currants and gooseberries, which only ripened during the hottest days of July. I found them absolutely useless for snacking, unlike the toothsome strawberries and raspberries, but pick them I did, hating the hot sun and gooseberry thorns. The currants would be juiced and prepared into jellies of jewel-like clarity. These were made in substantial amounts and graced our table throughout the year. In December jars of quince and currant jelly were tucked into Christmas boxes and sent off to relatives around the country. Gooseberries were for jam, and a few desserts including pies. It was gooseberry pie that one day built Mother's fame as a baker of renown. She had just pulled two gooseberry pies, with fine golden crusts, from the oven when there was a knock at the door. Friends had dropped by for a surprise visit. Folks used to do this on Sunday afternoon drives in the country. My parents invited them to stay for a cup of coffee and some gooseberry pie. Well, this couple had never before had gooseberry pie and the truth was Mother hadn't either. Forever after, when their group gathered if the conversation slowed Jim would begin waxing to anyone who would listen about Edith's gooseberry pies.

Mother grew strawberries and raspberries and any not eaten fresh were made into preserves. Each year some of our quinces and rose petals went to Anna, who was like an aunt to us all. With these she would make the translucent Greek preserves known as spoon sweets. These were later served in tiny spoonfuls on a saucer along with strong dark Greek coffee. She was one of the few Greeks in our town and a great friend of our family since my father, though born in Cleveland, was of Greek parentage. My Greek grandmother would regularly join us for long visits. She and Anna would together cook the wonderful foods of Greece, an amalgam of my grandmother's Athenian favorites and Anna's delights from Salonika. In summer we often ate outside and if Anna and her husband were with us, Anna would pronounce it a garden party. I would look around at all the flowers and shrubs in bloom and in my child's mind think yes, it is a garden and we're all here so I guess it is a garden party.

Grandmother was more of a gatherer than a gardener and adored collecting tiny bouquets of purple violets. She introduced us all to the fresh wild greens of spring. Here in Western Oregon, the fields are covered with the blooms of naturalized mustards for several months, from spring to early summer. Grandmother Nichols made a ritual of collecting wild greens. A version of spanakopita was made of tender mustard greens, combined with onions, eggs, dill, and feta cheese all blanketed with phyllo pastry. Greens and garlic were braised in olive oil and served with slices of lemon. Not only mustard grew in nearby fields but other greens such as nettles, and relatives of amaranth and she would prepare and serve them to us. One, we never forgot, was an ill chosen collection of young thistles, perhaps she thought they were cardoons or would be tender after boiling, but serve them forth she did. Around the table our eyes grew wide as the scratchy substance made its way down our throats. I didn't want to be disloyal but had to ask, "Grandma, is this really what they eat in Greece?" "No, they don't grow this way in Greece" was her sharp reply. We were never again served thistles but we later shared many a chuckle over it and we all appreciated how much my grandmother's love of being in a garden and around growing plants enriched our lives. I still think how fortunate I was to have had this wonderful cultural window opened to me at an early age. When I pick the herbs of Greek cuisine she used in abundance, the dill, bay, oregano, and spearmint, I think of her. Many years ago when our daughter was just a toddler, we were house hunting. We went around to the large backyard and Katie knelt in one of the many pools of blooming violets. I knew we were home.

In her later years Mother was stricken with severe rheumatoid arthritis. This once vigorous supple woman became increasingly imprisoned in her own body. Her gardening activities had to change. There was no longer such a need to provide food for the table and she and my father had a growing business that required constant attention. Gardening became an avenue for self-expression and she sought out interesting varieties and ornamentals that thrived in the Northwest. She had always grown lavender, now she had rows of it and made all sorts of potpourri and sachets from the dried flowers. Fragrant herbs were planted throughout her garden and because many are plants with a story she studied their lore and did more armchair gardening. Still each spring she would get out her books and catalogs and often announce "this year it will be a riot of color" and indeed it often was as she merrily combined a kaleidoscope of flowers with good result. She had a deck built off her kitchen and this is where she entertained friends and enjoyed sitting in the evening.

Upon returning from a family wedding in Greece she described her sister-in-law, Athena, picking lemons, tomatoes, and herbs, all from her small balcony garden. At home she was increasingly frustrated by her physical limitations and how they impeded her gardening. She could always ask people for help but what she really wanted was to put her own fingers in the dirt, plant her seeds, and do her own watering. So began a new excursion into the world of container gardening. Her deck provided the space and my husband, Keane, and I helped her set it up. A convenient potting table, a lever on her faucet for easy handling, and lots of handy ergonomically designed hand tools got her started. She had always loved growing white nicotiana starts for her friends and now she had several flats growing and could share them lavishly. Her tomatoes grew tall with good supports. Her beloved herbs grew close by her kitchen for easy collecting. Hot peppers and eggplants provided color and most importantly she had enough to share with friends. This opportunity to share was integral to her great pleasure in gardening. I shared her enjoyment and interest, finding varieties that would perform well, and became serious about container gardening myself. Once again she was seeking out new plants and excited to see a catalog offering strawberries that would grow as large as a peach. These she ordered and while not quite that large were productive good-looking plants.

I believe there is a mother-daughter dance that begins at birth when as a young mother we carry our babes around the kitchen singing and rhythmically moving and hoping they love the songs that come from our heart. Sometimes it seems we're partners in perfect synchronicity and other times almost a tug-of-war when we are trying too hard to teach in a time that is not a learning moment. My mother gardened all her life and I admired and appreciated what she did but I too wanted to garden for myself with my own successes and mistakes. Now my own daughter, a senior in college, is taking courses in landscape design, just for fun. She has not shown too keen an interest in gardening, so I happily listen as she describes her design and tells me how it creates a vista in a small garden. So it is with gardening, there's always another season and new gardeners budding forth.

CHAPTER 2

"In the Garden— Fond Memories of My Mother"

by Cathy Wilkinson Barash

I was blessed with four memorable gardening seasons with my mother; she died when I was five and a half years old. (As precocious as I was—there are snapshots of me in the garden at nine months of age—I don't start counting my gardening years until I was one year and nine months old.) Although our time together was short, my fondest memories are of the time we spent together at the beach and in the garden—back in the kinder, gentler, innocent days of the early 1950s.

My mother, father, and I lived in a small beach town off the south shore of Long Island, New York, one of a few year-round residents. The houses were quite close to each other—a driveway and garage on one side and about 10 feet on the other. Eight stairs led to the landing; sloped raised beds flanked the stairs.

Like most of the houses, the backyard consisted of a plain concrete slab abutting the house and garage. Daddy built a brick barbecue in one corner, with 3-foot-high brick walls along the two exposed sides. He added 2-foot-deep, brick-edged, raised beds along the wall and topped the walls with lattice. As a finishing touch, he painted everything white. This gave us just enough space—front and back—to have gardens that we could enjoy with little effort.

With spring came the vernal rituals, beginning with our annual outing to Atlantic Nursery. My mother and I strolled around and through the myriad displays of annuals; she lifted me up to see—and smell—the flowers I was too short to see. She made sure that we picked out "only the bestest plants." She held up each pot or flat so both of us could examine and sniff it. I can swear that fragrances were much richer and more distinct back in those days. She had a keen eye and a good nose, which I was blessed to inherit. Perhaps it was her expertise as an interior decorator that guided her to look beyond the color of the flowers at the other characteristics of the flower and plant: size, shape, form.

Back home, Mom set the wood flats on the shady side of the house by my "personal shower," the coiled garden hose with an adjustable nozzle. My mother demonstrated how to finely mist the plants—the same way I showered outdoors whenever we came home from the beach. I was so excited to have responsibility. The following morning, out we went to the back garden—pausing to look at our new plants and refresh our minds on their sizes, colors, and scents. I'd go into the garage and get out the 2-pound Chock Full O' Nuts coffee can in which we stored our garden tools—two trowels and a garden fork—and gloves.

A few roses graced the bed; a pale pink, lightly scented, climbing 'Cecile Brunner'; a richly perfumed, velvety, deep red 'Mister Lincoln'; and an even more richly perfumed, deeper red 'Mirandy'. No perennials; we created each year's unique look with annuals. We didn't use a lot of different types of flowers; we added interest by using several different varieties of the same plant—large pom-pom and feathery types—or a multicolor mix of verbena or petunias, as well as commingling plants.

Next came one of my favorite tasks: using the hand fork to loosen the soil and pull any errant weeds. My mother got me settled and went inside to make lemonade. The garden beds were a perfect fit for a small child, raised just enough that I could reach the back of the bed by kneeling on the brick edging. As I worked my way from one end of the garden to the other, breaking the crust of the soil, I found the rich, earthy aroma of the soil intoxicating. Often, before I reached to the end of the garden, I relinquished the fork and used my bare hands, it felt so good.

When I was almost done, Mom appeared with icy cold glasses of fresh lemonade, some crackers or cookies, and my metal beach pail and shovel. While I finished up, she'd dig out some garden soil and fill my pail with soil and add water from the hose. Somehow she knew exactly the right proportions of soil and water to make superb mud pies. Since my hands were already dirty, she'd put a straw—a special treat in those days—in my glass and held it so I could get a few sips. She got down on the ground with me; we made mud pies, and left them to bake on the patio. (Remember that this was an era in which women did not wear pants. Once the weather was warm enough, we spent a lot of time in bathing suits. From old slides and photos, it appeared that my mother had a complete wardrobe of bathing suits, and not nearly as many dresses or skirts. Fortunately, as a tot, I did get to wear shorts and pants around the house. By summer, I had a deep coppery, full-body tan—from running around all day in my topless bathing suit!) Our outdoor work was over for the day.

The following morning, I could barely contain my excitement; it was planting day! We headed out early in the morning, as my mother always said, "Plant early in the morning before the dew is off the ivy." In addition, the backyard was shaded for much of the morning. I misted the plants and she brought them to the garden. Cell packs would not come on the scene for another decade; we had half or quarter flats of pansies, marigolds, verbenas, and single pots of petunias and one or two other plants that varied from year to year.

Some of the books and articles I have written address garden design. If you promise not to tell, I'll let you in on a secret: I plant my garden in the same manner as my mother showed me fifty some years ago—no design, no plans. She placed the plants on the soil, moving them around until she had achieved a look that pleased her. My contribution was to disbud all the flowers just before she set each plant in the ground; she said that my small hands were just the right size for bud plucking without damaging any surrounding leaves. Once every plant was in the ground, I got to finish the planting process, pressing down the soil around each transplant.

As my mother picked up each plant, she showed me its unique characteristics—leaf shape and color, flower shape and color. It was not pedantic in any way, we found fun ways to describe the characteristics in terms of common items we knew. For example, the morning glories and moonflower were like a whirling Christmas toy. We rubbed the leaves to catch each one's unique scent and stuck our noses in the flowers—before I disbudded them. To this day, I can conjure up the sweet, slightly vanilla scent of the verbena. We rated the flowers, deciding that the purple flowers were the most fragrant, with red running a close second. Watering the garden was so much fun! Mom alternated between spraying me and the garden; that was the first time I saw a rainbow—in the gentle spray from the hose. It was "Mommy magic"; to this day I am heartbroken if I don't see a rainbow when I am watering the garden.

The front garden was a completely different matter. The slope was steep enough that my mom decreed it unsafe for us to get in and replant each year—except at sidewalk level. The beds were mirror images of each other, with the ubiquitous mophead hydrangea at the center of each. In beach towns in the 1950s, hydrangeas were de rigueur as they thrived in the sandy soil with little to no attention. Each year we tried a different way to get the hydrangeas to change from blue to pink. After three years, we actually succeeded, but we forgot what we had used to cause the change. The highlight of these beds was the showstopping display of spring-blooming bulbs in vibrant primary colors. Yellow daffodils followed purple crocus in succession. Then came the eye-catching orange, red, and yellow tulips. By the time the tulips finished blooming, the hydrangeas leafed out, filling much of the space. Here, I also got to be the garden assistant, helping plant the deep vivid red geraniums that Mom overwintered each year. I loved the salty, tangy scent of the leaves. I now wonder whether the limited choice of bulbs we had then didn't make gardens more impressive than the numerous types of bulbs in a wide range of colors that are available today.

On the indoor gardening front, I remember finding an incredibly fragrant, blooming hyacinth each year along with my Easter basket. I couldn't fathom how it could be growing—it was in a glass of water, no soil. The Easter bunny, Mom explained, had magical powers, and could even make a bulb bloom in water. One year, I came upon my mother in the basement, bent over a table with water-filled glasses that seemed to glow under the fluorescent lights, putting something that looked like a small purple potato atop each glass. I tried to sneak down the stairs without being heard, but mothers have a second sense, knowing when their progeny are mischievous nearby. Aghast, my bubble burst, was there no Easter bunny? Mom folded me into her arms, reassuring me that the Easter bunny was real. She went on to explain that since the Easter bunny had to make it all over the world in one night, unlike Santa who had his sled and reindeer to fly him around, the

Easter bunny needed some help to get all his deliveries made on time. Since there was an array of hyacinth bulbs in forcing glasses on the table, my mother easily convinced me that she was one of the Easter bunny's special helpers, growing hyacinths for lots of boys and girls. The Easter bunny picked up the flowers as he went around our neighborhood, leaving me the strongest, largest, most floriferous, and fragrant hyacinth of all. The purple ones were the hyacinths of choice. To this day, I get a strong craving for chocolate—in the form of a bunny—whenever I get a whiff of a hyacinth's perfume.

My mom was an excellent seamstress—a talent I have not inherited. Each year she made matching mother-daughter dresses for us to wear on Easter Sunday. Another yearly ritual: We sat on the front stoop as my dad photographed us, using two different cameras. One for black-and-white prints and the other for Kodachrome slides with colors that are as glowing today as they were fifty years ago.

As spring progressed, we spent more and more time in the backyard, watching the plants grow, set bud, and bloom. The day after Memorial Day was seed-planting day. After dinner on Memorial Day, my mother opened the seed packets of morning glories and moonflowers (night-blooming cousins of morning glories). The first year, she lifted me up so I could drop the seeds in the water—morning glories in one bowl and moonflowers in the other. The following year, I "accidentally" dropped all the seeds in one bowl. To Mom's surprise and my delight, the random planting actually looked better than when it was planned. In the morning, we went out and planted the seeds along the wall. Mom hung strings down from the lattice for the vines to climb the wall. I could see growth from day to day. As the vines grew and began to bloom, I was entranced. From my second-story bedroom, I could climb up on a chair and peer out at night. The sweet perfume of the moonflowers wafted towards me. I watched the heart-shaped leaves ripple with the breeze. Years later, I realized that the scene would not have caught my eye if the trellis was any color but white. The contrast between dark and light made the leaves visible; the iridescent white moonflower blooms stand out against the deep green leaves. More than likely, this experience planted the seeds of what would become my third book, *Evening Gardens*.

Throughout the summer, my father took photos of me in front of the back garden, in my best dress with white anklets and black patent leather Mary Janes. Often I was captured leaning into the garden, sniffing one of the roses. One year, something interrupted the photo session—Dad probably needed more film. As I had been sniffing around the garden, I must have wondered if the flowers tasted as good as they smelled. A willful child, I didn't ask anyone before I began nibbling some of the petals. "Mirandy" and "Mister Lincoln" roses were sweetly delectable; ferny little marigolds, lemony; big marigolds, yucky; nasturtiums, spicy; and portulacas were salty.

Mom came out as I was munching "Mister Lincoln"—half of the red petal in my mouth, and the other probably looking like a big blotch of blood. My mother freaked out and ran to me, yelling, "What happened? You're bleeding. Are you okay?" When she was close enough to see it wasn't blood, she asked what was in my mouth. I pointed to the rose. She ordered me to spit it out and I complied. She was shaking with anger and terror. What else had I eaten? I showed her. Mom calmed down a bit and tried to explain that flowers were not edible and I should never eat any more. Precocious as I was, I asked, "Says who?" Her reply was that she had said it, probably assuming it would end there. Being in the last month of the "terrible twos," I went on to ask how she knew that flowers were inedible. She gave the standard answer of that era, "They say so." I retorted, asking, "Who are they?" She hesitated and replied that "they" were the people who wrote books, in this case garden books and cookbooks. For the time being I was content with that answer; it's surprising how serene I look in the photo taken a few minutes later.

Fortunately, the flowers I sampled were not only safe to eat but grown without the use of chemicals. My guardian angel must have been watching over me. Had I chosen to eat a petunia or morning glory flower, I might not even have survived a ride to the hospital. Both Mom and Dad later confided that as children they had eaten clover blossoms when their fathers picked them in a field. One day, Mom and I found some red clover growing in an empty lot, and indeed, it was delicious—crunchy with a sweet honey flavor.

Years passed, yet the kernel of interest had been firmly planted in my mind. I looked for books about edible flowers. I found a few that were written in the 1970s and 1980s, many of which were written in England. To my mind, they left me with more questions than answers. The consistent fault in all the literature was the use of common names, but no botanical names. Since a plant can have numerous common names—varying from region to region and especially from country to country, there was no way to properly identify that two flowers with the same name were the same flower. A number of flowers are poisonous, so it's important to be sure of what you're eating.

I kept hearing my mother's words of wisdom, "If you can't find an answer to a question, it's a sign to look closer and discover it yourself." I started working on a book on edible flowers in 1984; it took five years to find a publisher. *Edible Flowers from Garden to Palate* came out in 1993, garnering several prestigious awards, including a nomination for the Julia Child cookbook award. It is considered the seminal book on the subject, including growing information, common and botanic names, ID photos of the 67 plants, and a total of 288 recipes with scrumptious photos. My inner child couldn't help chuckling with the immature, "Na na na na na, told you so!!" I also realized that I was now one of "them," I could pass on the joy of edible flowers to others.

Although our time together was too short, part of my mother is with me in any garden I create. Sometimes, I can almost feel her looking over my shoulder, guiding my hands as I tend my plants. Whenever I see a rainbow, I am momentarily transported back to early childhood: warm sunny days, lying on the chaise lounge, safe in my mother's arms, admiring our garden.

CHAPTER 3

"Letter to My Mother"

from *Small Wonder*

by Barbara Kingsolver

I imagine you putting on your glasses to read this letter. *Oh, Lord, what now?* You tilt your head back and hold the page away from you, your left hand flat on your chest, protecting your heart. "Dear Mom" at the top of a long, typed letter from me has so often meant trouble. Happy, uncomplicated things—these I could always toss you easily over the phone: I love you, where in the world is my birth certificate, what's in your zucchini casserole, happy birthday, this is our new phone number, we're having a baby in March, my plane comes in at seven, see you then, I love you.

The hard things went into letters. I started sending them from college, the kind of self-absorbed epistles that usually began as diary entries and should have stayed there. During those years I wore black boots from an army surplus store and a five-dollar haircut from a barbershop and went to some trouble to fill you in on the great freedom women could experience if only they would throw off the bondage of housewifely servitude. I made sideways remarks about how I couldn't imagine being anybody's wife. In my heart I believed that these letters—in which I tried to tell you how I'd become someone else entirely different from the child you'd known—would somehow make us friends. But instead they only brought me a few quick gulps of air while I paced out the distance between us.

I lived past college, and so did my hair, and slowly I learned the womanly art of turning down the volume. But I still missed you, and from my torment those awful letters bloomed now and then. I keep trying; I'm trying still. But this time I want to say before anything else: Don't worry. Let your breath out. I won't hurt you anymore. We measure the distance in miles now, and I don't have to show you I'm far from where I started. Increasingly, that distance seems irrelevant. I want to tell you what I remember.

* * *

I'm three years old. You've left me for the first time with your mother while you and Daddy took a trip. Grandmamma fed me cherries and showed me the secret of her hair: Five metal hairpins come out, and the everyday white coil drops in a silvery waterfall to the back of her knees. Her house smells like polished wooden stairs and soap and Granddad's onions and ice cream, and I would love to stay there always but I miss you bitterly without end. On the day of your return I'm standing in the driveway waiting when the station wagon pulls up. You jump out your side, my mother in happy red lipstick and red earrings, pushing back your dark hair from the shoulder of your white sleeveless blouse, turning so your red skirt swirls like a rose with the perfect promise of *you* emerging from the center. So beautiful. You raise one hand in a tranquil wave and move so slowly up the driveway that your body seems to be underwater. I understand with a shock that you are extremely happy. I have been miserable and alone waiting in the driveway, and you were at the beach with Daddy and *happy*. Happy without me.

I am sitting on your lap, and you are crying. *Thank you, honey, thank you,* you keep saying, rocking back and forth as you hold me in the kitchen chair. I've brought you flowers: the sweet peas you must have spent all spring trying to grow, training them up the trellis in the yard. You had nothing to work with but abundant gray rains and the patience of a young wife at home with pots and pans and small children, trying to create just one beautiful thing, something to take you out of our tiny white clapboard house on East Main. I never noticed until all at once they burst through the trellis in a pink red purple dazzle. A finger-painting of colors humming against the blue air: I could think of nothing but to bring it to you. I climbed up the wooden trellis and picked the flowers. Every one. They are gone already, wilting in my hand as you hold me close in the potato-smelling kitchen, and your tears are damp in my hair but you never say a single thing but *Thank you.*

Your mother is dead. She was alive, so thin that Granddad bought her a tiny dark-blue dress and called her his fashion model and then they all went to the hospital and came home without her. Where is the dark-blue dress now? I find myself wondering, until it comes to me that they probably buried her in it. It's under the ground with her. There are so many things I don't want to think about that I can't bear going to bed at night.

It's too hot to sleep. My long hair wraps around me, grasping like tentacles. My brother and sister and I have made up our beds on cots on the porch, where it's supposed to be cooler. They are breathing in careless sleep on either side of me, and I am under the dark cemetery ground with Grandmamma. I am in the stars, desolate, searching out the end of the universe and time. I am trying to imagine how long forever is, because that is how long I will be dead for someday. I won't be able to stand so much time being nothing, thinking of nothing. I've spent many nights like this, fearing sleep. Hating being awake.

I get up, barefoot and almost nothing in my nightgown, and creep to your room. The door is open, and I see that you're awake, too, sitting up on the edge of your bed. I can make out only the white outline of your nightgown and your eyes. You're like a ghost.

Mama, I don't want to die.

You don't have to worry about that for a long, long time.

I know. But I'm thinking about it now.

I step toward you from the doorway, and you fold me into your arms. You are real, my mother in scent and substance, and I still fit perfectly in your lap.

You don't know what Heaven is like. It might be full of beautiful flowers.

When I close my eyes I discover it's there, an endless field of flowers. Columbines, blue asters, daises, sweet peas, zinnias: one single flower bed stretching out for miles in every direction. I am small enough to watch the butterflies come. I know them from the pasture behind our house, the butterflies you taught me to love and name: monarchs, Dianas, tiger swallowtails. I follow their lazy zigzag as they visit each flower, as many flowers as there are stars in the universe. We stay there in the dark for a long time, you and I, both of us with our eyes closed, watching the butterflies drift so slowly, filling as much time as forever.

I will keep that field of flowers. It doesn't matter that I won't always believe in Heaven. I will suffer losses of faith, of love and confidence, I will have some bitter years, and always when I hurt and can't sleep I will close my eyes and wait for your butterflies to arrive.

CHAPTER 4

"My Mother's Flower Garden"

from *The Souvenir of Western Women*

by Charlotte Matheny Kirkwood

My mother, Mary Cooper Matheny, spent her childhood and youth under the vine-clad arbors of an old Kentucky home, flowers, vines, and trees her constant companions. In preparing to come westward she carefully gathered seeds from flowers and shrubs. These she brought across the plains. Mother's seed sack occupied the safest corner in wagon or tent. After leaving the wagons at The Dalles, she carried her seed sack at the horn of her saddle through the Cascade Mountains to Oregon City, where the company arrived November 8, 1843.

In the spring of '44 my mother planted some of her seeds on a plot of ground near the present site of the town of Hillsboro. Later in the season my father bought a farm on the Willamette River just opposite the old Methodist Mission, then in ruins. To this place mother removed her flowers, and also planted other seeds. The result exceeded expectations; her garden became a dream of beauty. All the sweet old-fashioned favorites vied with each other in the blending of brilliant hues; throngs of gaily tinted butterflies and emerald and bronze humming birds reveled in the perfume-laden breath of pinks and roses.

Of the pinks she had a fine collection. The second year, when they began to bloom, she carefully culled the plants, saving only the most perfect. This she continued to do until her pinks in size and beauty were almost equal to the modern carnation. Also she rescued the old Mission Rose from the ruins of the mission, where it was having a hard fight to maintain its standard over native brush and bramble, as the only living representative of the civilized home. It blooms today in my own garden.

Among her collection were seeds of the old English sweet brier, prized for the beauty and fragrance of its foliage as well as for its dainty flowers and scarlet berries. A beautiful hedge shrub in some countries, but kissed by the bright sun and warm rains of Oregon, its elsewhere gentle nature has developed qualities most aggressive. Borne on the wings of bird and bee, it now presses its long prickly branches into the depths of our forests and along our lanes from the Willamette to the Pacific.

My mother was justly proud of her garden, for it was the first real flower garden in all this Northwest country. Many a plant and seed has been carried from it to brighten other homes throughout the Willamette Valley. Travelers always stopped to admire Mother's flowers and engage seeds for next year's planting, which she gave a free-will offering. Today a scion from the old historic Mission Rose sheds its fragrance upon her narrow bed in the cemetery near her home on the banks of the Willamette.

Chapter 5

"The Butterfly Garden"

by Louise Hallberg

The Hallberg Ranch has been in my family since 1883. In the 1920s butterflies became frequent visitors to our garden, thanks to my mother's love for planting flowers.

At that time, my sister and I were in grammar school at Oak Grove, studying birds and flowers. In those days, many of the flowers in our garden were started by seeds or cuttings. On a visit to my aunt, my mother spotted a pipe-shaped flower growing on a vine along the side of the road—it would later be identified as Dutchman's Pipevine. She secured a cutting, which we shared with classmates and planted in our flower garden.

Since then, this vine has flourished, spreading throughout the garden around our family home. We learned that Dutchman's Pipevine attracts the beautiful black and iridescent blue butterfly, the Pipevine Swallowtail, which lays its eggs on this vine in order to provide its hatching caterpillars with their only food source.

After I retired in 1975, I began noticing more and more Pipevine Swallowtails frequenting our garden. In 1990, with the recommendation and encouragement of a local arboretum, I actively planted additional varieties of host and nectar plants to attract and welcome more species of butterflies.

My mother's flower gardens became a nonprofit organization known as Hallberg Butterfly Gardens in 1997. It's a haven to over forty species of butterflies throughout the year. On sunny, warm days, Monarchs, Painted Ladies, Red Admirals, Mourning Cloaks, Buckeyes, and several species of little skippers can be sighted nectaring on flowers and flying about.

The gardens are open to the public by appointment April through October, with an Open Gardens Day in June. Tours are conducted for school children; most are in kindergarten through second grade. Some can even walk to the gardens from the grammer school I attended; others come from neighboring cities and counties, visit on field trips, or come with their families. Gardening clubs and enthusiasts also frequent our tours. Those not familiar with a butterfly's life cycle are awed by the information they receive. I remember one woman commenting after her tour, "I think I'll be more careful not to harm the caterpillars," because she had seen the beautiful butterflies they become!

Last year alone (not counting the butterflies) we had over 1,750 visitors. Some people come specifically to see the butterflies; others come to take in the unique flower gardens, acquiring ideas to attract butterflies to their own gardens. In 2000, Gay Bishop Brorstrom wrote a children's book about the gardens, illustrated by Kathy Goetzel. This past summer, grandmothers visited with their grandchildren—the children had all received the book and their grandmothers wanted them to visit and experience the gardens firsthand!

My mother and I seldom discussed the butterflies, the fruits of her labor. I cherish two butterfly books she was given, but her real interest and love was flowers—particularly wildflowers. Her flourishing flower and wildflower gardens led to my love for the butterflies they attract. This year, I will be eighty-eight years young, and I hope to continue sharing my passion, the Hallberg Butterfly Gardens, with our visitors through tours; enjoying the continual planting, weeding, and watering in the gardens; and sighting the magical butterflies.

CHAPTER 6

"The Single Mom"

from *An Obsession With Butterflies*

by Sharman Apt Russell

You are weighty. You are filled with eggs. Your abdomen drags you toward the earth.

You have wonderful eyesight, and you are proud of that: your wonderful compound eye made of hundreds of smaller eyes, each with its own lens. You are able, simultaneously, to see up, down, forward, and backwards. You can see all the colors—red, orange, yellow, green, blue, purple, plus ultraviolet, plus all the colors mixed with ultraviolet, purple and ultraviolet, blue and ultraviolet, green and ultraviolet. You don't easily adjust for distance or see detailed patterns and shapes. But you know and recognize two very important shapes: You know the broad, oval leaves of the Texas Dutchman's pipe and the narrow, grass-like leaves of the Virginia snakeroot.

In the pine woodlands of east Texas, where you live, you are searching for these sprawling, wild, perennial herbs. Both have small, purple-brown, bad-smelling flowers, the better to attract pollinators such as flies and carrion beetles. Both are the host plants of your larvae who eat the leaves and absorb the aristolochic acids that make them unpalatable to bird. Slowly, you fly above the grasses, herbs, and shrubs, looking for the leaf shape you like best.

Today you like broad ovals. Last time you laid eggs, you used a broad oval leaf, and now broad oval leaves are all you can think about. They are your idée fixe.

In fact, it is March, and you are just beginning to lay eggs, and the broad oval leaves of Texas Dutchman's pipe are more abundant than the narrow leaves of Virginia snakeroot. Later in the season, you may switch to a different shape. Your willingness to change is good, since the broad leaves of Dutchman's pipe grow tough as they age, become hard to digest, poor in nitrogen. Your larvae could starve on such a plant. Virginia snakeroot, however, is always tender, even in May.

If you were capable of love, you would love your larvae

dearly, with all your long, tiny, kinked heart, with all the instincts of your seed-sized brain. At the same time, your particular caterpillars are not the easiest ones in the world to care for. It's not their fault. You're not blaming them.

You blame the host plant. It's too small. Your voracious eating machines eat it up and then have to eat a new one. Sometimes a larva has to find and consume fifty plants before it can successfully pupate. The first plant, the plant you are searching for now, is the most important. The larger your larva is when it leaves the plant, the greater chance it has to survive.

Patiently, you fly about the grasses, herbs, and shrubs, looking for the leaf shape you like best and smelling for the odor of your host plant with your antenna, with the top of your head, with parts of your wings. Over and over, you land on a broad oval leaf. You tap the leaf with your foot.

You are proud of your feet, too, which have taste organs that can zero in on sugar as quickly as a third grader. When your feet taste something sweet, you lower your proboscis, ready to feed.

When you tap or drum a leaf with your foreleg, you are testing for the chemicals in your host plant. Because you are female, your forelegs are designed to support repeated strong strokes. On each foreleg is a cluster of sensory hairs that look like a tiny toothbrush. Spines on the tip of your forelegs may also pierce the leaf's skin so that juices and odors can flow to these hairs.

You drum, and in less than half a second, you know that this broad oval leaf is not the right broad oval leaf, not a Texas Dutchman's pipe but some other plant. You don't feel surprised. This is what usually happens. You spend most of your life on the wrong leaf.

You fly off. You land. You drum.

You fly off. You land. You drum.

You keep drumming.

Yes. Yes, this tastes right! This smells right. This is your larvae's host plant.

You stop drumming and look around. You are searching for eggs. If there are too many caterpillars on one plant, your larvae won't have enough food. They might start eating each other.

Now you see them: four reddish brown humps. In a matter of hours, tiny purple-brown caterpillars will break out of these humps. They will eat their shells and begin to eat whatever else they can find, feeding together in a group until they are larger.

You fly off in disgust.

You land. You drum. You fly off. You land. You drum. You fly off. You land. You drum.

You keep drumming. You stop. You look for reddish brown humps. This time, there are none. This time, the plant is perfect.

You fly off again.

You are a Pipevine Swallowtail, and it is still a mystery why and when you decide to lay your eggs.

You have a relative in Japan, another swallowtail, who determines the density of her host plant by landing on a certain number of them in a certain time frame. Her clutch size of eggs varies depending on that information. If there are a lot of host plants in the area, she will lay a lot of eggs; if there are not many host plants, she will lay fewer eggs.

You may be doing this, or you may not.

You are, in any event, taking your time, trying to be selective, and you feel smug about that. You know skippers who let their eggs drop haphazardly so that they fall anywhere about the plant. You know of Marbled Whites and Ringlets who broadcast their eggs while flying!

You don't pretend to be the perfect mother. For example, your larvae would survive better in a shady habitat than in a sunny one. But you still look for host plants in the sun and lay your eggs there. In this way, you avoid being eaten by orb-weaving spiders. Also, you need heat for your flight muscles to reach the right temperature, heat to generate energy to fly and search and fly and drum. (In another climate, you might worry more that fungal infections might kill your eggs, and you would reject any place too damp or dismal.)

At times, you stop your search to sip nectar from a flower.

You are attracted to the colors pink and purple. You bask by spreading your wings and letting them radiate heat into the air under and around your body. You avoid or reject males who want to mate.

You fly. You land. You drum. You fly. You land. You drum. Finally, on a Texas Dutchman's pipe free of eggs, you throw caution to the wind. "*Que sera, sera,*" you hum impetuously.

You are weighty, filled with eggs, and you are ready to lay this burden down.

You curve your abdomen toward the leaf and position your ovipositor, the rounded end of a tube through which the eggs travel singly and are fertilized by sperm stored in your spermatophore. Your ovipositor has taste and sensory hairs that evaluate the site one more time. It may have simple eyes that further guide you.

You're like a driver backing her car out of a tight spot. You're like a pilot landing her aircraft on a naval ship. Careful, careful. Over here. Over here. Down. Put her down.

You have another important decision to make. You usually lay from two to five eggs. If this plant has a lot of leaves, if it seems young and healthy, you may tend toward the larger number. You may lay more eggs, too, if you haven't laid any in a long time, if you are feeling, perhaps, an uncomfortable urgency.

You decide to lay three eggs and you secrete a glue that attaches them to the underside of a leaf. It takes you about a minute. You fly off, and you don't look back. You've done your part. You will lay hundreds of eggs before you die. How many of these survive, if any survive, will depend largely on the site you have chosen for them.

You have tried hard to balance the selection of that site with your own needs and with the pressure of time.

It hasn't been easy.

You're not complaining.

You don't expect any thanks.

CHAPTER 7

"A River of Sunlight"

by Sharon Lovejoy

My earliest memories are of Grandmother Lovejoy in her sunny cottage garden, where the days seemed endless and the star-flecked nights were always warm and thick with the perfume of jasmine and gardenias.

Grandmother smelled like the carnations under the peach tree and the sweet peas that tumbled over the lattice arbor. Her speckled hands, which could coax life from the tiniest seed or the most unlikely cutting, resembled the gnarled roots of the guava tree that clutched the sandy hillside. Her wispy silver hair always refused to remain under the brim of her straw hat and looked as fly-away and gossamer as the thistle-down that drifted above the garden. She was as soft as a ripened fig, and she had a voice that could sound as whispery as rustling sycamore leaves or prickle like blades of St. Augustine grass on bare feet.

Our family's tiny redwood house nestled into an orchard of apricot and peach trees just steps from Grandmother's old bungalow. A dense privet hedge—the safe haven for scores of birds—surrounded our homes and shielded them from the view of passersby.

Grandmother's garden blazed with the colors of her prizewinning bearded iris, gladiolas, and battalions of paint-box hued hollyhocks and chocolate-faced sunflowers. Small doilies of glaucous-leaved California poppies and purple heart-sease insinuated their way into every crevice and crack of the terrace. Tiny mats of dianthus, alyssum, and thyme limned the borders, crept onto the pathways, and released their scent whenever we brushed past. Even with my eyes closed, I could tell where Grandmother worked by the aromatic trail of flowers and herbs that followed her.

Her tidy kitchen plot stood in the lee of a tangled wall of boysenberries that sheltered and fed a night-singing mocking-bird. Fig, guava, and avocado trees skirted with circular beds of lettuce, cabbage, tomatoes, and herbs provided us (and a shy resident opossum) with fresh food for our meals and a surplus of goods for pies, chutneys, jams, and candied fruits. Every morning, Grandmother and I set aside a few quiet minutes to walk the pathways and check on the well-being of our plants. This intimate time in our yard not only helped us to catch problems as they appeared, but also taught us about Mother Nature's workforce, which has a natural series of checks and balances that are complex, self-sustaining, and a constant source of wonder.

Early one morning, we found that hundreds of looper caterpillars had attacked our cabbages and made lace work of their leaves. Despite our efforts, the chore of getting rid of these pests seemed impossible. The amber-eyed mockingbird, who kept a vigilant watch over everything that went on in "his" yard, kibitzed at us from his hiding place in the boysenberries. As we searched the beds for the loopers, the mocker scissored through the air, landed in the midst of our tattered crop, and picked through the leaves like a shopper at a tag sale. Within minutes, he had plucked and eaten dozens of the pests, far more than we could gather in a day of hard work.

Our garden hummed with life. Iridescent Anna's hummingbirds scolded from their twiggy perches in the scarlet bottlebrush. Gold-belted bumblebees nuzzled into the hearts of heavenly blue morning glories and rolled around like kittens in a patch of catnip. Topaz and carnelian dragonflies patrolled the skies above the beds and borders, their wings clicking castanet style in their quick skirmishes. The dark-winged mourning cloak butterflies lit on our bare arms and tasted us as though we were flowers. Grandmother's garden was never about work, but always about the magic that surrounded us every minute we were outdoors. Ours was a secret world in a river of sunlight and fragrance.

The sight of Grandmother's broad back bent over her beds of flowers is how I most clearly remember her. As she knelt she patted the soil, plucked any weeds that dared to invade her borders, and talked lovingly to her flowers and trees the way a mother would speak to her child. She congratulated them on the beauty of their fruits and flowers and discussed the tribulations of aphid infestations and spider mites. Whenever she reached out to pick a flower or fruit, she would pause, ask permission, and then thank the plant for its offerings of beauty and food.

Most gardeners concentrate on feeding their plants a regimen of store-bought fertilizers, but Grandmother's methods were strictly homemade. She had a three-part recipe for her land that we tested and improved through our years together.

One of our recipe's ingredients came from Mr. Brown, our next-door neighbor. He was famous for his chickens and for his double-yolked eggs. When we visited him, we almost never returned home with something for breakfast or dinner, but we always had a load of chicken manure for our garden. Grandmother taught me that a piece of ground needs food as surely as a growing child or a hungry animal.

Our kitchen scraps were an important part of our garden's diet. We tossed everything from coffee grounds to leftover piecrust into a drainer in the sink and dumped the contents into our tall compost pile. Leaves, grass clippings, and trimmings were mixed with our garbage. The tower of compost settled and sank until it was a short mound that steamed like a teakettle on a low flame. We could reach into the pile, and if it felt as warm as just-baked bread, we knew it was cooking and would soon be done to perfection.

When our compost was reduced to a dark and unrecognizable heap of mulch, we spread it around our vegetables and fruit trees and onto the flower beds. Our plants and trees looked as though we had swaddled them in a fluffy brown comforter.

The secret ingredient that Grandmother added to her soil was also the one that made me the happiest. Through the hot months of summer, I looked forward to a harvest that could only happen when the first wild rains of autumn swept into our valley.

Our homes sat at the bottom of a steep road that coursed with water and mud slides after each heavy downpour. As soon as we could venture outdoors, Grandmother and I would don our raincoats and boots and trudge along the sidewalks in search of stranded earthworms. We plucked them from the mud as gently as farmers harvesting saffron strands, and dropped them into our rescue buckets. In just a short time, we gathered skeins of displaced (and very lucky) worms and headed home to our garden.

We wished the worms good luck as we "sowed" them into potted plants and throughout our beds and borders. Grandmother taught me that those slender wigglers produced castings as good for the soil as Mr. Brown's chicken manure. I learned that as our refugee worms ate their way through the earth they created a network of tunnels that made it easy for plant roots, air, and water to move through the soil.

Even the tiniest chore outdoors became a joyous adventure when I shared it with my Grandmother Lovejoy. I didn't realize that our days together could end abruptly and forever. After all, I was a child and believed in the fairy tales we read aloud under the sheltering branches of our sycamore. On the day Grandmother died, I ran to the hidden playhouse under our guava trees and stayed inside it for hours. Nearby the mockingbird sang from the boysenberries, dragonflies clashed in the cloudless sky above me, and the Anna's hummingbird dipped into the fuchsias that draped over the pathway. I couldn't understand how all these things that we had loved and watched together could continue as though nothing had happened.

My world changed that day, but now I understand that my joyous times in Grandmother's garden formed my entire life. She gave me the gift of wonder, and I will pass that on to my own grandchildren with the hope that they will have their own secret world and a river of sunlight and fragrance.

Abigail Baker Lovejoy's Famous Candied Figs

September 1952

Wash fruit and cook gently in water for 1½ hours or so until done.

Drain overnight.

Cook fruit in syrup made with 2 cups of granulated sugar to each cup water (make sure the figs are covered with the syrup).

Cover pot and cook 1½ hours—let stand overnight.

Bring ingredients to a boil and cook another ½ hour (your figs will have a glazed look).

Place figs on a tray and dry in the sun or in a 250-degree preheated oven for 2 hours.

When figs are dry, roll them in a bowl of powdered sugar.

Place figs and some halved pecans in a covered container.

CHAPTER 8

"It's Mother!"

from *The Secret Garden*

by Frances Hodgson Burnett

Their belief in the Magic was an abiding thing. After the morning's incantations Colin sometimes gave them Magic lectures.

"I like to do it," he explained, "because when I grow up and make great scientific discoveries I shall be obliged to lecture about them and so this is practice. I can only give short lectures now because I am very young, and besides Ben Weatherstaff would feel as if he were in church and he would go to sleep."

"Th' best thing about lecturin'," said Ben, "is that a chap can get up an' say aught he pleases an' no other chap can answer him back. I wouldn't be agen' lecturin' a bit mysel' sometimes."

But when Colin held forth under his tree old Ben fixed devouring eyes on him and kept them there. He looked him over with critical affection. It was not so much the lecture which interested him as the legs which looked straighter and stronger each day, the boyish head which held itself up so well, the once sharp chin and hollow cheeks which had filled and rounded out and the eyes which had begun to hold the light he remembered in another pair. Sometimes when Colin felt Ben's earnest gaze meant that he was much impressed he wondered what he was reflecting on and once when he had seemed quite entranced he questioned him.

"What are you thinking about, Ben Weatherstaff?" he asked.

"I was thinkin'," answered Ben, "as I'd warrant tha's gone up three or four pound this week. I was lookin' at tha' calves an' tha' shoulders. I'd like to get thee on a pair o' scales."

"It's the Magic and—and Mrs. Sowerby's buns and milk and things," said Colin. "You see the scientific experiment has succeeded."

That morning Dickon was too late to hear the lecture. When he came he was ruddy with running and his funny face looked more twinkling than usual. As they had a good deal of weeding to do after the rains they fell to work. They always had plenty to do after a warm deep sinking rain. The moisture which was good for the flowers was also good for the weeds which thrust up tiny blades of grass and points of leaves which must be pulled up before their roots took too firm hold. Colin was as good at weeding as any one in these days and he could lecture while he was doing it. "The Magic works best when you work, yourself," he said this morning. "You can feel it in your bones and muscles. I am going to read books about bones and muscles, but I am going to write a book about Magic. I am making it up now. I keep finding out things."

It was not very long after he had said this that he laid down his trowel and stood up on his feet. He had been silent for several minutes and they had seen that he was thinking out lectures, as he often did. When he dropped his trowel and stood upright it seemed to Mary and Dickon as if a sudden strong thought had made him do it. He stretched himself out to his tallest height and he threw out his arms exultantly. Color glowed in his face and his strange eyes widened with joyfulness. All at once he had realized something to the full.

"Mary! Dickon!" he cried. "Just look at me!"

They stopped their weeding and looked at him.

"Do you remember that first morning you brought me in here?" he demanded.

Dickon was looking at him very hard. Being an animal

charmer he could see more things than most people could and many of them were things he never talked about. He saw some of them now in this boy. "Aye, that we do," he answered.

Mary looked hard too, but she said nothing.

"Just this minute," said Colin, "all at once I remembered it myself—when I looked at my hand digging with the trowel—and I had to stand up on my feet to see if it was real. And it is real! I'm well—I'm well!"

"Aye, that th' art!" said Dickon.

"I'm well! I'm well!" said Colin again, and his face went quite red all over.

He had known it before in a way, he had hoped it and felt it and thought about it, but just at that minute something had rushed all through him—a sort of rapturous belief and realization and it had been so strong that he could not help calling out.

"I shall live forever and ever and ever!" he cried grandly. "I shall find out thousands and thousands of things. I shall find out about people and creatures and everything that grows—like Dickon—and I shall never stop making Magic. I'm well! I'm well! I feel—I feel as if I want to shout out something—something thankful, joyful!"

Ben Weatherstaff, who had been working near a rose-bush, glanced round at him.

"Tha' might sing th' Doxology," he suggested in his dryest

grunt. He had no opinion of the Doxology and he did not make the suggestion with any particular reverence.

But Colin was of an exploring mind and he knew nothing about the Doxology.

"What is that?" he inquired.

"Dickon can sing it for thee, I'll warrant," replied Ben Weatherstaff.

Dickon answered with his all-perceiving animal charmer's smile.

"They sing it i' church," he said. "Mother says she believes th' skylarks sings it when they gets up i' th' mornin'."

"If she says that, it must be a nice song," Colin answered. "I've never been in a church myself. I was always too ill. Sing it, Dickon. I want to hear it."

Dickon was quite simple and unaffected about it. He understood what Colin felt better than Colin did himself. He understood by a sort of instinct so natural that he did not know it was understanding. He pulled off his cap and looked round still smiling.

"Tha' must take off tha' cap," he said to Colin, "an' so mun tha', Ben—an' tha' mun stand up, tha' knows."

Colin took off his cap and the sun shone on and warmed his thick hair as he watched Dickon intently. Ben Weatherstaff scrambled up from his knees and bared his head too with a sort of puzzled half-resentful look on his old face as if he didn't know exactly why he was doing this remarkable thing.

Dickon stood out among the trees and rose-bushes and began to sing in quite a simple matter-of-fact way and in a nice strong boy voice:

> *"Praise God from whom all blessings flow,*
> *Praise Him all creatures here below,*
> *Praise Him above ye Heavenly Host,*
> *Praise Father, Son, and Holy Ghost.*
> *Amen."*

When he had finished, Ben Weatherstaff was standing quite still with his jaws set obstinately but with a disturbed look in his eyes fixed on Colin. Colin's face was thoughtful and appreciative.

"It is a very nice song," he said. "I like it. Perhaps it means just what I mean when I want to shout out that I am thankful to the Magic." He stopped and thought in a puzzled way. "Perhaps they are both the same thing. How can we know the exact names of everything? Sing it again, Dickon. Let us try, Mary. I want to sing it, too. It's my song. How does it begin? 'Praise God from whom all blessings flow'?"

And they sang it again, and Mary and Colin lifted their voices as musically as they could and Dickon's swelled quite loud and beautiful—and at the second line Ben Weatherstaff raspingly cleared his throat and at the third line he joined in with such vigor that it seemed almost savage and when the "Amen" came to an end Mary observed that the very same thing had happened to him which had happened when he found out that Colin was not a cripple—his chin was twitching and he was staring and winking and his leathery old cheeks were wet.

"I never seed no sense in th' Doxology afore," he said hoarsely, "but I may change my mind i' time. I should say tha'd gone up five pound this week Mester Colin—five on 'em!"

Colin was looking across the garden at something attracting his attention and his expression had become a startled one.

"Who is coming in here?" he said quickly. "Who is it?"

The door in the ivied wall had been pushed gently open and a woman had entered. She had come in with the last line of their song and she had stood still listening and looking at them. With the ivy behind her, the sunlight drifting through the trees and dappling her long blue cloak, and her nice fresh face smiling across the greenery she was rather like a softly colored illustration in one of Colin's books. She had wonderful affectionate eyes which seemed to take everything in—all of them, even Ben Weatherstaff and the "creatures" and every flower that was in bloom. Unexpectedly as she had appeared, not one of them felt that she was an intruder at all. Dickon's eyes lighted like lamps.

"It's mother—that's who it is!" he cried and went across the grass at a run.

Colin began to move toward her, too, and Mary went with him. They both felt their pulses beat faster.

"It's mother!" Dickon said again when they met halfway. "I knowed tha' wanted to see her an' I told her where th' door was hid."

Colin held out his hand with a sort of flushed royal shyness but his eyes quite devoured her face.

"Even when I was ill I wanted to see you," he said, "you and Dickon and the secret garden. I'd never wanted to see any one or anything before."

The sight of his uplifted face brought about a sudden change in her own. She flushed and the corners of her mouth shook and a mist seemed to sweep over her eyes.

"Eh! dear lad!" she broke out tremulously. "Eh! dear lad!" as if she had not known she were going to say it. She did not say, "Mester Colin," but just "dear lad" quite suddenly. She might have said it to Dickon in the same way if she had seen something in his face which touched her. Colin liked it.

"Are you surprised because I am so well?" he asked. She put her hand on his shoulder and smiled the mist out of her eyes. "Aye, that I am!" she said; "but tha'rt so like thy mother tha' made my heart jump."

"Do you think," said Colin a little awkwardly, "that will make my father like me?"

"Aye, for sure, dear lad," she answered and she gave his shoulder a soft quick pat. "He mun come home—he mun come home."

"Susan Sowerby," said Ben Weatherstaff, getting close to her. "Look at th' lad's legs, wilt tha'? They was like drumsticks i' stockin' two month' ago—an' I heard folk tell as they was bandy an' knock-kneed both at th' same time. Look at 'em now!"

Susan Sowerby laughed a comfortable laugh.

"They're goin' to be fine strong lad's legs in a bit," she said. "Let him go on playin' an' workin' in the garden an' eatin' hearty an' drinkin' plenty o' good sweet milk an' there'll not be a finer pair i' Yorkshire, thank God for it."

She put both hands on Mistress Mary's shoulders and looked her little face over in a motherly fashion.

"An' thee, too!" she said. "Tha'rt grown near as hearty as our 'Lisabeth Ellen. I'll warrant tha'rt like thy mother too. Our Martha told me as Mrs. Medlock heard she was a pretty woman. Tha'lt be like a blush rose when tha' grows up, my little lass, bless thee."

She did not mention that when Martha came home on her "day out" and described the plain sallow child she had said that she had no confidence whatever in what Mrs. Medlock had heard. "It doesn't stand to reason that a pretty woman could be th' mother o' such a fou' little lass," she had added obstinately.

Mary had not had time to pay much attention to her changing face. She had only known that she looked "different" and seemed to have a great deal more hair and that it was growing very fast. But remembering her pleasure in looking at the Mem Sahib in the past she was glad to hear that she might some day look like her.

Susan Sowerby went round their garden with them and was told the whole story of it and shown every bush and tree which had come alive. Colin walked on one side of her and Mary on the other. Each of them kept looking up at her comfortable rosy face, secretly curious about the delightful feeling she gave them—a sort of warm, supported feeling. It seemed as if she understood them as Dickon understood his "creatures." She stooped over the flowers and talked about them as if they were children. Soot followed her and once or twice cawed at her and flew upon her shoulder as if it were Dickon's. When they told her about the robin and the first flight of the young ones she laughed a motherly little mellow laugh in her throat.

"I suppose learnin' 'em to fly is like learnin' children to walk, but I'm feared I should be all in a worrit if mine had wings instead o' legs," she said.

It was because she seemed such a wonderful woman in her

nice moorland cottage way that at last she was told about the Magic.

"Do you believe in Magic?" asked Colin after he had explained about Indian fakirs. "I do hope you do."

"That I do, lad," she answered. "I never knowed it by that name but what does th' name matter? I warrant they call it a different name i' France an' a different one i' Germany. Th' same thing as set th' seeds swellin' an' th' sun shinin' made thee a well lad an' it's th' Good Thing. It isn't like us poor fools as think it matters if us is called out of our names. Th' Big Good Thing doesn't stop to worrit, bless thee. It goes on makin' worlds by th' million—worlds like us. Never thee stop believin' in th' Big Good Thing an' knowin' th' world's full of it—an' call it what tha' likes. Tha' wert singin' to it when I come into th' garden."

"I felt so joyful," said Colin, opening his beautiful strange eyes at her. "Suddenly I felt how different I was—how strong my arms and legs were, you know—and how I could dig and stand—and I jumped up and wanted to shout out something to anything that would listen."

"Th' Magic listened when tha' sung th' Doxology. It would ha' listened to anything tha'd sung. It was th' joy that mattered. Eh! lad, lad—what's names to th' Joy Maker," and she gave his shoulders a quick soft pat again.

She had packed a basket which held a regular feast this morning, and when the hungry hour came and Dickon brought it out from its hiding place, she sat down with them under their tree and watched them devour their food, laughing and quite gloating over their appetites. She was full of fun and made them laugh at all sorts of odd things. She told them stories in broad Yorkshire and taught them new words. She laughed as if she could not help it when they told her of the increasing difficulty there was in pretending that Colin was still a fretful invalid.

"You see, we can't help laughing nearly all the time when we are together," explained Colin. "And it doesn't sound ill at all. We try to choke it back but it will burst out and that sounds worse than ever."

"There's one thing that comes into my mind so often," said Mary, "and I can scarcely ever hold in when I think of it suddenly. I keep thinking suppose Colin's face should get to look like a full moon. It isn't like one yet but he gets a tiny bit fatter every day—and suppose some morning it should look like one—what should we do!"

"Bless us all, I can see tha' has a good bit o' play actin' to do," said Susan Sowerby. "But tha' won't have to keep it up much longer. Mester Craven'll come home."

"Do you think he will?" asked Colin. "Why?"

Susan Sowerby chuckled softly.

"I suppose it 'ud nigh break thy heart if he found out before tha' told him in tha' own way," she said. "Tha's laid awake nights plannin' it."

"I couldn't bear any one else to tell him," said Colin. "I think about different ways every day, I think now I just want to run into his room." "That'd be a fine start for him," said Susan Sowerby. "I'd like to see his face, lad. I would that! He mun come back—that he mun."

One of the things they talked of was the visit they were to make to her cottage. They planned it all. They were to drive over the moor and lunch out of doors among the heather. They would see all the twelve children and Dickon's garden and would not come back until they were tired.

Susan Sowerby got up at last to return to the house and Mrs. Medlock. It was time for Colin to be wheeled back also. But before he got into his chair he stood quite close to Susan and fixed his eyes on her with a kind of bewildered adoration and he suddenly caught hold of the fold of her blue cloak and held it fast.

"You are just what I—what I wanted," he said. "I wish you were my mother—as well as Dickon's!"

All at once Susan Sowerby bent down and drew him with her warm arms close against the bosom under the blue cloak—

as if he had been Dickon's brother. The quick mist swept over her eyes.

"Eh! dear lad!" she said. "Thy own mother's in this 'ere very garden, I do believe. She couldna' keep out of it. Thy father mun come back to thee—he mun!"

CHAPTER 9

"Smell the Roses"

from *Around the House and in the Garden*

by Dominique Browning

One summer my younger son informs me that, come September, I will no longer be permitted to walk him to school. Actually, Theo has been gently preparing me for months, dropping big fat hints that he can no longer afford to indulge me in this time together. He knows our morning walks are one of my favorite things, but he is painfully aware that no one else in the fifth grade goes to school with his mother, certainly no one holds hands with his mother or gets a kiss at the corner.

Though he has been equally reluctant to say good-bye, as middle school looms a walk with Mom is just out of the question.

It is almost impossible to let go of that little hand. Of course, Theo has had just as much trouble as I have. Those early morning walks—how did they come to mean so much to us? They began, of course, out of necessity. We could have driven to school, but I refused to do that; the school is too close. Eventually I understood that we needed the slow start to the day: the foot-dragging; the whining and complaining (about cold, heat, hunger, sun, rain, nightmares, piano lessons, breakfast); the review of life's small outrages (perpetrated by his brother, his cousins, his friends, his enemies, girls, rabbis, piano teachers).

I came to see that my morning job was to listen, and as there was nothing acceptable to say about Theo's troubles, I began to insert garden instruction into his litany of woes. "I can't believe I have to go to a piano lesson this afternoon," he would begin. "My entire life is ruined and I have scheduling stress." (Apparently the school day now includes classes on how to handle stress, a concept I had never even heard of when I was his age, during which children are taught to put their fingertips together and breathe deeply while they discuss "strategies to avoid riding the conflict escalator.")

"Look, darling, there are Mr. So-and-so's new French tulips," I would reply. "What an amazing shade of orange, and what a great idea, to mix them in with the daffodils. Isn't that beautiful, the way the low morning sun glows through them?" This would be met with a grunt, a new complaint. "Do I really have to take piano lessons? Why can't I take guitar lessons? Why can't I take no lessons?" "And look at the carpet of purple, Theo. That's ajuga, and it's spreading through the lawn." "Sure, Mom." "Those red flowers are camellias, my love. They don't normally grow so well this far north." "Okay, right, whatever, Mom."

And on it goes. Braced for his apathy about the gardens, I plow ahead, partly to counterpoint his aggrieved morning airs and partly out of a belief that if I give him the names of the things in the gardens as we walk by, he will eventually care about the things themselves and grow up to be a gardener. So I persist, and he does, too—"I'm doomed, Mom." "Those roses, Theo dear."—down the street, around the corner, up a few blocks, pointing out mosses embedded in cracks in the sidewalks, honeysuckle, irises, lilac, wisteria, peonies, and of course, pines, maples, oaks, sassafras, pears, beeches. We will stop, and I'll poke at a shrub or prod an ant across a mossy knoll, and he'll shiver or groan or sag under the weight of his backpack, and in this way we will the delay the inevitable arrival at school until we're more or less ready to let each other go.

Every morning—for years now—my son has responded to my garden enthusiasms with a little attitude of bemusement, as if to say, "There, there, dear, you'll be fine." He knows the drill so well that if I skip the commentary about a particular patch of moss or someone's hedge, he will squeeze my hand and hesitate expectantly at the spot. But he also assures me he will never remember any of the names. "You're wasting your breath, Mom."

Still, I know it won't be lost on him. Many years ago, in Texas, I heard an old man say to a harried reporter, "Son, you're living life like a clenched fist." I did not want this to be visited upon my son. Who gardens with a clenched fist? Gardens slow things down, relax that death grip with which we grasp the time we are given. I want simply to teach my children to see the roses. One day they will know enough to stop and smell them, too.

CHAPTER 10

"Stardust Tomatoes in the Kitchen Window"

by Doreen G. Howard

It was the day before the first hard freeze was expected in the fall of 1948 when Gram emptied her garden and introduced me to the growing power of stardust. My dad, an Army Air Corp pilot, was stationed in occupied Germany after World War II. And, my mom and I were living temporarily with her parents at the family farm, on the Red River north of Paris, Texas. My world was filled with hard-working adults who lived by the natural rhythm of crop and livestock cycles. They had little time to entertain an inquisitive four-year-old. The only playmates I had were two cats and an ornery rooster who squawked and tried to peck me every time I ventured beyond the back door. Gram realized how isolated I was and used her gardening skills to make my world brighter.

That fall day, she stripped all the tomato vines of their green fruit in the garden behind the two-story house where Mom, Gram, and her father were all born and raised. The quarter-acre plot had fed four generations and still produced all the vegetables we ate. She made putting the garden to bed an adventure, enlisting my help to find all the green tomatoes remaining on plants. Gram wrapped each pale green globe in newspaper and placed them in boxes to be stored in the pantry for ripening. My job was to rip newspaper sheets in quarters and hand them to her. Soon I was covered in ink smudges and had leaves in my pigtails from crawling under the vines to find the last hidden tomatoes. "There are enough tomatoes in the boxes to take us through January," Gram announced as we finished. "But it will be June until we see another fresh one—unless I plant kitchen tomatoes."

"*Kitchen* tomatoes?" My mind, primed by nightly fairy tales filled with magic brooms, pumpkins which became coaches, and clocks that talked, envisioned vines snaking around the tin sink, over the water pump, and across to the wood-burning cook stove in Gram's comfortable turn-of-the-century kitchen!

I had dreadful visions of the vines swallowing the cats and lassoing my hands as I fell asleep near the warm stove while watching bread bake, my usual Saturday afternoon practice.

Gram, of course, had something else in mind. She pushed tiny seeds into four pots full of garden dirt and placed them on the kitchen windowsill. Then she tied back the curtains so the pots would receive plenty of light in the south-facing window. By Thanksgiving, the kitchen tomatoes were eighteen inches high and producing their first flowers. It was my daily job to gently shake the tiny yellow blooms—"just like the bees do outside," Gram explained, "and like the fairies do when they sprinkle stardust."

Before long, Christmas was upon us. Gram and Mom filled the house with delicious aromas from the fruitcakes, stollen, and cookies they baked. Granddad and I went to a neighbor's wood lot and cut down a bushy white pine that added more intoxicating fragrance to the house. We decorated the tree with oranges studded with cloves and rolled in freshly ground cinnamon, and gingerbread boy cookies. Granddad put five white paper stars I cut from shirt boxes amongst the pine boughs. And, we sprinkled silver glitter on the tree, because Gram said glitter attracted fairies. I figured they would like our tree so much that they might leave a magical gift or two. It worked! One arrived on Christmas Eve from Germany. It was an enormous parcel containing a porcelain doll with long, flaxen ringlets from Dad. He sent chocolate coins wrapped in gold foil, too, and an embroidered blouse for Mom. We showed our exotic treasures to the steady stream of visitors who shared our holidays. With all the festivities, the tomatoes faded from my mind . . . until the first snowfall on New Year's Day brought me back to the kitchen window.

"Gram," I shouted, "it's magic! The plants grew ten feet overnight. Fairies must have sprinkled stardust on them!" I was a big fan of stardust, constantly pestering Gram and Mom to read a well-worn copy of *Peter Pan* to me.

My grandmother chuckled. "It could be them, now that you mention it. Fairies love tomatoes almost as much as good boys and girls. And, stardust would make the plants get big enough in a hurry to make tomatoes."

Five days went by. I inspected the plants every hour to see if there were any tiny tomatoes. My patience was nearly exhausted when I spied the first one. More appeared every day, and I practiced counting by tallying the tomatoes every morning. Afternoons were spent with Gram basking in the brightness of the window and warming our hands with hot cocoa while we admired the pale green fruits as they put on size. She sat in her overstuffed chair, between the stove and window, read stories out loud from the *Saturday Evening Post*, and told tales of when she was a girl.

In the middle of January, seed catalogs that were more fascinating than *Saturday Evening Post* started arriving in the mail. Brilliantly colored flowers and vegetables leaped off of every page. Gram patiently explained that we could order seeds, the mailman would deliver them to our post box at the end of the road, and when spring arrived we could plant the seeds in the garden. I wanted to order everything! Reminding me of our limited budget, Gram said I could pick one flower and one vegetable for the spring garden. It was an impossible task. I wanted everything. Finally, I chose red and white candy-striped zinnias and yellow pear-shaped tomatoes. I figured they would ripen faster than the sluggish ones that languished on our kitchen windowsill, because they didn't have to turn red to be ripe.

After Gram placed her seed orders, she suggested that I take a pair of scissors to the vivid pictures in the catalogs. I carefully snipped sweet peas, delphinium, larkspur, carnations, marigolds, and more. Then, with a paste she concocted with flour and water, I glued my paper garden all over an old cigar box Granddad found in the cellar. What a wonderful surprise it would make for Mom, I thought. She recently found a job in Paris, twenty-seven miles away, and worked long hours, arriving home tired and glum every evening. The colorful flower garden box would cheer her up, and she could keep the weekly letters from my dad in it. They were now in her top dresser drawer in a stack tied with a pale blue ribbon.

The kitchen tomatoes soon stretched my patience, as my focus turned back to the kitchen window. They were turning red ever so S-L-O-W-L-Y. There hadn't been a tomato for dinner in over a month, and I loved them. I desperately wanted a thick slice on a piece of homemade honey wheat bread slathered with butter made from our cow's milk. Couldn't those fairies speed up the magical process?

Finally, the day came when Gram picked the first ripe, red tomato. The occasion coincided happily with Valentine's Day, which is when I planned to give Mom the flower garden box. That evening Gram and I presented Mom with a tray that held the tomato and my box when she arrived home from work. "Oh, Mama," she exclaimed, wiping tears from her eyes. "Kitchen tomatoes! And the most beautiful box in the world from my daughter," she sobbed, patting my homemade present. "They almost make me forget that Lou is still in Germany and how I miss him." I was upset that Mom was crying until Gram took me aside to explain that Mom's tears were because we made her happy.

We ate kitchen tomatoes at lunch and dinner for weeks. Sometimes, there was only one ripe, but Gram sliced it thinly so everyone could have a bite. Meanwhile, she cleared space on the windowsill for six tiny pots of dirt in which she planted more tomato seeds. They sprouted, grew rapidly, and were set in the garden during the second week of April, along with the kitchen tomatoes, which kept on producing more juicy red globes. Shortly after Gram's outdoor tomatoes started ripening in June, my dad returned from Germany. His visit was short, and he went back to an Army base in El Paso to await release from the military. Three months later, we were permanently reunited as a family and moved to Fort Worth, where Dad had a job waiting as a test pilot for an aircraft company.

Nearly every Christmas afterwards, for as long as my grandparents lived, we spent the holiday at the family farm. The house always smelled heavenly from the cakes and cookies Gram baked. And Granddad still cut down a fragrant pine we covered with clove-studded oranges rolled in cinnamon, and gingerbread boys and silver glitter. But, there were never tomatoes in the kitchen window again. Mom said it was because Gram didn't have a little girl to shake the flowers.

Today, the grandmother is me. My sunny kitchen window is filled with tomato plants every winter, and I have a granddaughter—with her own visions of fairies—who loves to shake the flowers. There's one difference. I plant tomato varieties like Silvery Fir Tree, Early Girl, and Red Robin that ripen their fruit fast. You see, I recall exactly how impatient a little girl can be, even when fairies spread stardust.

CHAPTER 11

"Inside the Garden Gate"

from *Mother Stories*

by Maud Lindsay

PART I

Grandmother's garden was a beautiful place—more beautiful than all the shop windows in the city; for there was a flower or grass for every color in the rainbow, with great white lilies, standing up so straight and tall, to remind you that a whole rainbow of light was needed to make them so pure and white.

There were pinks and marigolds and princes' feathers,

with bachelor's buttons and Johnny-jump-ups to keep them company. There were gay poppies and gaudy tulips, and large important peonies and fine Duchess roses in pink satin dresses.

There were soft velvet pansies and tall blue flags, and broad ribbon grasses that the fairies might have used for sashes; and mint and thyme and balm and rosemary everywhere, to make the garden sweet; so it was no wonder that every year the garden was full of visitors.

Nobody noticed these visitors but Grandmother and Lindsay.

Lindsay was a very small boy, and Grandmother was a very old lady; but they loved the same things, and always watched for these little visitors, who came in the early spring-time and stayed all summer with Grandmother.

Early, early in the spring, when the garden was bursting into bloom in the warm Southern sunshine, Grandmother and Lindsay would sit in the arbor, where the vines crept over and over in a tangle of bloom, and listen to a serenade. Music, music everywhere! Over their heads, behind their backs, the little brown bees would fly, singing their song:

"Hum, hum, hum!
Off and away!

To get some
Sweet honey to-day!"

while they found the golden honey cups, and filled their pockets with honey to store away in their waxen boxes at home.

One day, while Grandmother and Lindsay were watching, a little brown bee flew away with his treasure, and lighting on a rose, met with a cousin, a lovely yellow butterfly.

"I think they must be talking to each other," said Grandmother, softly. "They are cousins, because they belong to the great insect family, just as your papa and Uncle Bob and Aunt Emma and Cousin Rachel all belong to one family, the Greys; and I think they must be talking about the honey that they both love so well."

"I wish I could talk to a butterfly," said Lindsay, longingly; and Grandmother laughed.

"Play that I am a butterfly," she proposed. "What color shall I be—a great yellow butterfly, with brown spots on my wings?"

So Grandmother played that she was a great yellow butterfly with brown spots on its wings, and she said to Lindsay:

"Never in the world can you tell, little boy, what I used to be?"

"A baby butterfly," guessed Lindsay.

"Guess again," said the butterfly.

"A flower, perhaps; for you are so lovely," declared Lindsay, gallantly.

"No, indeed!" answered the butterfly; "I was a creeping, crawling caterpillar."

"Now, Grandmother, you're joking!" cried Lindsay, forgetting that Grandmother was a butterfly.

"Not I," said the butterfly. "I was a crawling, creeping caterpillar, and I fed on leaves in your Grandmother's garden until I got ready to spin my nest; and then I wrapped myself up so well that you would never have known me for a caterpillar; and when I came out in the Spring I was a lovely butterfly."

"How beautiful!" said Lindsay. "Grandmother, let us count the butterflies in your garden." But they never could do that, though they saw brown and blue and red and white and yellow ones, and followed them everywhere.

PART II

It might have been the very next day that Grandmother took her knitting to the summer house. At all events it was very soon; and while she and Lindsay were wondering when the red rose bush would be in full bloom, Lindsay saw, close up to the roof, a queer little house, like a roll of crumpled paper, with a great many front doors; and, of course, he wanted to know who lived there.

"You must not knock at any of those front doors," advised Grandmother, "because Mrs. Wasp lives there, and might not understand; although if you let her alone she will not hurt you. Just let me tell you something about her."

So Lindsay listened while Grandmother told the story:

Once there was a little elf, who lived in the heart of a bright red rose, just like the roses we have been talking about.

There were many other elves who lived in the garden. One, who lived in a lily which made a lovely home; and a poppy elf, who was always sleepy; but the rose elf liked her own sweet smelling room, with its crimson curtains, best of all.

Now the rose elf had a very dear friend, a little girl named Polly. She could not speak to her, for fairies can only talk to people like you and me in dreams and fancies, but she loved Polly very much, and would lie in her beautiful rose room, and listen to Polly's singing, till her heart was glad.

One day as she listened she said to herself, "If I cannot speak to Polly, I can write her a letter"; and this pleased her so much that she called over to the lily elf to ask what she should write it on. "I always write my letters on rose petals, and get the wind to take them," said the rose elf. "But I am afraid Polly would not understand that."

"I will tell you," answered the lily elf, "what I would do. I would go right to Mrs. Wasp, and ask her to give me a piece of paper."

"But Mrs. Wasp is very cross, I've heard," said the rose elf timidly.

"Never believe the gossip that you hear. If Mrs. Wasp does seem to be a little stingy, I'm sure she has a good heart," replied the lily elf. So the rose elf took courage, and flew to Mrs. Wasp's house, where, by good fortune, she found Mrs. Wasp at home.

"Good morning, Mrs. Wasp," called the little elf, "I've come to see if you will kindly let me have a sheet of paper to-day."

"Now," said the wasp, "I have just papered my house with the last bit of paper I had, but if you can wait, I will make you a sheet."

Then the rose elf knew that Mrs. Wasp had a kind heart; and she waited and watched with a great deal of interest while Mrs. Wasp set to work. Now, close by her house was an old bit of dry wood, and Mrs. Wasp sawed it into fine bits, like thread, with her two sharp saws that she carries about her. Then she wet these bits well with some glue from her mouth, and rolled them into a round ball.

"Oh, Mrs. Wasp!" cried the rose elf, "I'm afraid I am putting you to too much trouble."

"Don't fret about me," said the wasp; "I'm used to work."

So she spread out the ball, working with all her might, into a thin sheet of gray paper; and when it was dry, she gave it to the rose elf.

"Thank you, good Mrs. Wasp," said the elf; and she flew away to invite the lily elf and the poppy elf to help her with the letter, for she wanted it to be as sweet as all the flowers of spring.

When it was finished they read it aloud.

"Dear Polly:
I'm a little elf;
I live within a flow'r;
I love to hear your happy song,
It cheers my ev'ry hour.
That I love you, I'd like to say
To you, before I close,
And please sing sweetly ev'ry day
To
Your friend within a Rose."

The letter was sent by a bluebird; and the elf was sure that Polly understood, for that very day she came and stood among the flowers to sing the very sweetest song she knew.

PART III

Out in Grandmother's garden, just as the sun was up, a very cunning spinner spun a lovely wheel of fine beautiful threads; and when Grandmother and Lindsay came out, they spied it fastened up in a rose bush.

The small, cunning spinner was climbing a silken rope near by with her eight nimble legs, and looking out at the world with her eight tiny eyes, when Grandmother saw her and pointed her out to Lindsay; and Lindsay said:

"Oh, Mrs. Spider! come spin me some lace!" which made Grandmother think of a little story which she had told Lindsay's papa and all of her little children, when they were lads and lassies, and this garden of hers had just begun to bloom.

She sat down on the steps and told it to Lindsay.

Once, long, long ago, when the silver moon was shining up in the sky, and the small golden stars were twinkling, twinkling, a little fairy with a bundle of dreams went hurrying home to fairyland.

She looked up at the stars and moon to see what time it was, for the fairy queen had bidden her come back before the day dawned.

All out in the world it was sleepy time; and the night wind

was singing an old sweet lullaby, and the mocking bird was singing too, by himself, in the wood.

"I shall not be late," said the fairy, as she flew like thistle-down through the air or tripped over the heads of the flowers; but in her haste she flew into a spider's web, which held her so fast that, although she struggled again and again, she could not get free.

Her bundle of dreams fell out of her arms, and lay on the ground under the rose-bush; and the poor little fairy burst into tears, for she knew that daylight always spoiled dreams, and these were very lovely ones.

Her shining wings were tangled in the web, her hands were chained, and her feet were helpless; so she had to lie still and wait for the day time which, after all, came too soon.

As soon as the sun was up, Mrs. Spider came out of her den; and when she saw the fairy she was very glad, for she thought she had caught a new kind of fly.

"If you please, Mrs. Spider," cried the fairy quickly, "I am only a little fairy, and flew into your web last night on my way home to fairyland."

"A fairy!" said Mrs. Spider crossly, for she was disappointed; "I suppose you are the one who helps the flies to get away from me. You see well enough then!"

"I help them because they are in trouble," answered the fairy gently.

"So are you, now," snapped the spider, "but the flies won't help you."

"But perhaps you will," pleaded the fairy.

"Perhaps I won't," said the spider, going back into her house and leaving the little fairy, who felt very sorrowful.

Her tears fell like dew drops on the spider web, and the sun shone on them, and made them as bright as the fairy queen's diamonds.

The fairy began to think of the queen and the court, and the bundle of dreams; and she wondered who would do the work if she never got free. The fairy queen had always trusted her, and had sent her on many errands.

Once she had been sent to free a mocking bird that had been shut in a cage. She remembered how he sang in his cage, although he was longing for his green tree tops.

She smiled through her tears when she thought of this, and said to herself:

"I can be singing, too! It is better than crying."

Then she began to sing one of her fairy songs:

"Oh! listen well, and I will tell,
Of the land where the fairies dwell;
The lily bells ring clear and sweet,

And grass grows green beneath your feet
In the land where the fairies dwell,
In the land where the fairies dwell."

Now though the fairy did not know it, Mrs. Spider was very fond of music; and when she heard the sweet song, she came out to listen. The little fairy did not see her, so she sang on:

"Grasshoppers gay, by night and day,
Keep ugly goblins far away
From the land where the fairies dwell,
From the land where the fairies dwell."

Mrs. Spider came a little farther out, while the fairy sang:

"There's love, sweet love, for one and all—
For love is best for great and small—
In the land where the fairies dwell,
In the land where the fairies dwell."

Just as the fairy finished the song she looked up, and there was Mrs. Spider, who had come out in a hurry.

"The flies are not going to help you," said she, "so I will," and she showed the fairy how to break the slender threads, until she was untangled and could fly away through the sunshine.

"What can I do for you, dear Mrs. Spider?" the fairy asked, as she picked up her bundle of dreams.

"Sing me a song sometimes," replied Mrs. Spider. But the fairy did more than that; for soon after she reached fairyland, the fairy queen needed some fine lace to wear on her dress at a grand ball.

"Fly into the world," she said, "and find me a spinner; and tell her that when she has spun the lace, she may come to the ball and sit at the queen's table."

As soon as the fairy heard this, she thought of the spider, and made haste to find her and tell her the queen's message.

"Will there be music?" asked the spider.

"The sweetest ever heard," answered the fairy; and the spider began to spin.

The lace was so lovely when it was finished, that the fairy queen made the spider court spinner; and then the spider heard the fairies sing every day, and she too had love in her heart.

PART IV

A mocking bird sang in Grandmother's garden. He was king of the garden, and the rose was queen. Every night when the garden was still, he serenaded Grandmother; and she would lie awake and listen to him, for she said he told her all the glad tidings of the day, and helped her understand the flower folk and bird folk and insect folk that lived in her garden.

Lindsay always thought the mocking bird told Grandmother the wonderful stories she knew, and he wanted to hear them, too, late in the night time; but he never could keep awake. So he had to be contented with the mocking bird in the morning, when he was so saucy.

There were orioles and thrushes and bluebirds, big chattering jays, sleek brown sparrows, and red-capped woodpeckers; but not a bird in the garden was so gay and sweet and loving as the mocking bird, who could sing everybody's song and his own song, too.

Night after night he sang his own song in Grandmother's garden. But there came a night when he did not sing; and though Grandmother and Lindsay listened all next day, and looked in every tree for him, he could not be found.

"I'm afraid somebody has caught him and shut him up in a cage," said Grandmother; and when Lindsay heard this he was very miserable; for he knew that somewhere in the garden, there was a nest and a mother bird waiting.

He and Grandmother talked until bedtime about it, and early next morning Lindsay asked Grandmother to let him go to look for the bird.

"Please do, Grandmother," he begged. "If somebody has him in a cage I shall be sure to find him; and I will take my own silver quarter to buy him back."

So after breakfast Grandmother kissed him and let him go, and he ran down the path and out of the garden gate, and asked at every house on the street:

"Is there a mocking bird in a cage here?"

This made people laugh, but Lindsay did not care. By and by, he came to a little house with green blinds; and the little lady who came to the door did not laugh at all when she answered his question:

"No; there are no mocking birds here; but there are two sweet yellow canaries. Won't you come in to see them?"

"I will sometime, thank you, if Grandmother will let me," said Lindsay; "but not to-day; for if that mocking bird is in a cage, I know he's in a hurry to get out."

Then he hurried on to the next house, and the next; but no mocking birds were to be found. After he had walked a long way, he began to be afraid that he should have to go home, when, right before him, in the window of a little house, he saw a wooden box with slats across the side; and in the box was a very miserable mocking bird!

"Hurrah! hurrah!" cried Lindsay, as he ran up the steps and knocked at the door. A great big boy came to the window and put his head out to see what was wanted.

"Please, please," said Lindsay, dancing up and down on the doorstep, "I've come to buy the mocking bird; and I've a whole silver quarter to give for it, because I think maybe he is the very one that sang in Grandmother's garden."

"I don't want to sell it," answered the boy, with a frown on his face.

Lindsay had never thought of anything like this, and his face grew grave; but he went bravely on:

"Oh! but you will sell it, maybe. Won't you, please? Because I just know it wants to get out. You wouldn't like to be in a cage yourself, you know, if you had been living in a garden—'specially my Grandmother's."

"This bird ain't for sale," repeated the boy, crossly, frowning still more over the bird-cage.

"But God didn't make mocking birds for cages," cried Lindsay, choking a little. "So it really isn't yours."

"I'd like to know why it isn't," said the boy. "You'd better get off my doorstep and go home to your Granny, for I'm not going to sell my mocking bird—not one bit of it"; and he drew his head back from the window and left Lindsay out on the doorstep.

Poor little Lindsay! He was not certain that it was the bird, but he was sure that mocking birds were not meant for cages; and he put the quarter back in his pocket and took out his handkerchief to wipe away the tears that would fall.

All the way home he thought of it and sobbed to himself, and he walked through the garden gate almost into Grandmother's arms before he saw her, and burst into tears when she spoke to him.

"Poor little boy!" said Grandmother, when she had heard all about it; "and poor big boy, who didn't know how to be kind! Perhaps the mocking bird will help him, and, after all, it will be for the best."

Grandmother was almost crying herself, when a click at the gate made them both start and then look at each other; for there, coming up the walk, was a great big boy with a torn straw hat, and with a small wooden box in his hand, which made Lindsay scream with delight, for in that box was a very miserable-looking mocking bird.

"Guess it is yours," said the boy, holding the box in front of him, "for I trapped it out in the road back of here. I never thought of mocking birds being so much account, and I hated to make him cry."

"There now," cried Lindsay, jumping up to get the silver quarter out of his pocket. "He is just like Mrs. Wasp, isn't he, Grandmother?" But the boy had gone down the walk and over the gate without waiting for anything, although Lindsay ran after him and called.

Lindsay and Grandmother were so excited that they did

not know what to do. They looked out of the gate after the boy, then at each other, and then at the bird.

Lindsay ran to get the hatchet, but he was so excited with joy that he could not use it, so Grandmother had to pry up the slats, one by one; and every time one was lifted, Lindsay would jump up and down and clap his hands, and say, "Oh, Grandmother!"

At last, the very last slat was raised; and then, in a moment, the mocking bird flew up, up, up into the maple tree, and Lindsay and Grandmother kissed each other for joy.

Oh! everything was glad in the garden. The breezes played pranks, and blew the syringa petals to the ground, and up in the tallest trees the birds had a concert. Orioles, bluebirds, and thrushes, chattering jays, sleek brown sparrows, and red-capped woodpeckers, were all of them singing for Grandmother and Lindsay; but the sweetest singer was the mocking bird who was singing everybody's sweet song, and then his own, which was the sweetest of all.

"I know he is glad," Lindsay said to Grandmother; "for it is, oh, so beautiful to live inside your garden gate!"

Chapter 12

"To Any Reader"

from *A Child's Garden of Verses*

by Robert Louis Stevenson

As from the house your mother sees
You playing round the garden trees,
So you may see, if you will look
Through the windows of this book,
Another child, far, far away,
And in another garden, play.
But do not think you can at all,
By knocking on the window, call

That child to hear you. He intent
Is all on his play-business bent.
He does not hear; he will not look,
Nor yet be lured out of this book.
For, long ago, the truth to say,
He has grown up and gone away,
And it is but a child of air
That lingers in the garden there.

CHAPTER 13

"Gardening with Louise"

by Judith B. Tankard

My mother was a pistol. Everyone who knew Louise considered her a character. She always spoke her mind, especially in later years when her tongue rolled forth with a flow of admonishments about people not doing things "right." She thought nothing of writing letters—"I wrote a blister of a letter today," she'd announce—to complain of poor service or other slights. Her favorite targets were department stores, mainly B. Altman, Arnold Constable, and Lord & Taylor, who occasionally let her down by sending the wrong item or failing to give her prompt credit. I'll never forget the letter she once wrote to White Flower Farm, complaining about their being out of some daffodils she'd ordered a bit late in the season. I had given her a gift certificate for her birthday in the hopes that she'd treat herself to one of those fragrant hanging jasmine plants illustrated in their catalog. Instead she decided to order daffodils and was furious to learn that they planned to send them for the following year. No amount of reasoning on my part would convince her that it wasn't their fault.

Life at home was not always easy. My father had a low boiling point and his rants and raves frequently sent my cats and friends running for cover. His sneezing fits (which I inherited) rattled the walls of the house. He was a lawyer and dominated dinnertime conversation with his daily trials and tribulations, some of which, in retrospect, were fascinating. Not surprisingly, my mother kept busy with many activities centered around her friends, church, and garden clubs. In the halcyon days of the 1950s when I was growing up, my mother eagerly looked forward to having her regular bridge group over for gossip, drinks, and specially baked treats. When an angel food cake or other confection appeared fresh from the oven on the appointed day, she'd warn us, "I'm saving that for the bridge club this afternoon."

It was in her garden that Louise, like many other women, found her solace. This is when she was the calmest and seemed to enjoy life the most. Her garden was her pride and joy, and years later I inherited her trusty old copy of Taylor's *Garden Encyclopedia* and various books and pamphlets on begonias and houseplants. She didn't talk much about gardening, at least when I was within earshot, but I have vivid images of her digging in the garden, covered in dirt and clad in shorts and a bright bandana stylishly wrapped around her head. For my mother, one of the happiest days of the year was the arrival of a truckload of steaming manure destined for her rose beds and dumped rather unceremoniously in the middle of the backyard.

Louise had three gardens during her lifetime, but I remember little about the first one in a small rowhouse in Queens, New York. Family snapshots show a tiny yard filled with beds of iris and annuals, all of which I seem to have taken a shine to. The house was always decked out with houseplants and vases of flowers (one of which I knocked over, my mother told me, reaching out of my playpen). Perhaps this is where the spark of gardening all began for me?

When I was four years old, we moved to Brightwaters, then a storybook village on the South Shore of Long Island. This was the home that Louise threw her heart into and where we lived for the next ten years. Like many suburban gardens of the 1950s, it had wavy-edged borders enclosing the backyard, with a teardrop-shaped rose garden to one side. Louise's garden was filled with lilacs, beds of iris, and, in the spring, hundreds of daffodils. In the center of the lawn was her beloved clothes line, with sheets, towels, and underwear flapping in the breeze. Back in those days it fell to me to iron the sheets by a system of clever folds, now a long-lost art.

The front yard was simpler, mostly yews and other foundation plantings hugging the white stucco house, but tucked away in one corner was a bed of primroses. Reluctantly my mother had to destroy these plants when the family doctor pronounced that I was allergic to them. Oddly, my mother never encouraged me to garden nor did she set aside an area for me to grow things. This was her style in the kitchen too, even to the end of her days; she liked doing things herself without any help (except dishwashing) and consequently I never learned to cook until I was on my own after college.

After living in the house a few years, my mother had a small greenhouse built outside her kitchen window so she could raise African violets, begonias, and seedlings. Throughout the year, our sunporch was a jungle of houseplants and, in late winter, pots of amaryllis. When I was a kid, I spent a lot of time at the dentist. These appointments, of course, were to be dreaded, but out of all of this my mother received a bonanza. She convinced our dentist to save the tiny glass vials that the novocaine came in so that she could use them for waterproof plant labels; a tiny cork at one end of the vial held the handwritten label she carefully inserted inside. It was a clever idea and I always wondered if she read about it in *Good Housekeeping* or *Woman's Day*.

In addition to gardening, Louise's activities branched out to all manner of postwar home economics, including flower arranging, canning, and later freezing. She joined the local ladies home bureau where she learned tailoring (she was an expert seamstress), lampshade-making, rug-hooking, and glove-making, among other things. She made all my father's ties (the proper way, on the bias with lamb's wool interlining) and knitted his socks. Of course she made all my clothes. As a youngster, I posed in the garden with my mother in our matching outfits, or shelled peas properly decked out in a gingham sunsuit and sunbonnet. She made all our Easter outfits, but by the time I was a teenager I was mortified by these creations and longed to dress like my friends.

Not all my memories about Louise's garden are pleasant. On one occasion, while showing the girl next door one of my mother's prized begonias, I inadvertently knocked the blossom off. Later that afternoon, while I was taking my required nap, my father stomped into my bedroom and dragged me out to the garden to "explain" what happened. Ever since then, I've hated begonias; in fact, I cannot even look at them straight in the eye. My mother also made me collect Japanese beetles from her rose bushes, paying me a penny for each one I dropped into a bottle of kerosene. I've never much liked tea roses either, and it wasn't until I visited the glorious gardens of England years later that I learned to love other types of roses. I still don't have them in my garden, though.

After ten years in our Long Island paradise, we moved back to New York City because my father found the daily commute from Long Island to Wall Street taxing. We settled into Forest Hills Gardens in Queens, not far from where we had lived before and where my parents lived for over thirty years. Understandably, my mother was not happy about moving back to the city and I, just fourteen years old, was faced with the prospect of making new friends. It didn't help matters that my father had begun collecting clocks in earnest—dozens of them would ding on the hour, much to the astonishment of my friends during overnight pajama parties. And the house was furnished with frightening Victorian furniture, including a parlor organ, that was so unlike the more comfortable homes of my classmates.

Despite being plucked away from her suburban paradise, my mother quickly made a new garden in our new backyard. The house was only seventeen feet wide and the yard not quite that deep, and it was surrounded on three sides by high hedges that my father clipped. As far as I know, this and mowing the postage-stamp-sized lawn were his only responsibilities in the garden. Within this minuscule framework, Louise had a year-round floral show, starting with dozens of daffodils and tulips in late spring and progressing to a medley of daylilies, roses, lupins, and herbs in the summer. Large tomato plants vied with the ubiquitous clothes line in the center of the yard.

The sunporch in the Forest Hills house was filled to bursting with dozens of hanging plants, tiers of African violets, and many forbidding-looking cacti. Most prized among the plants was my grandmother's night-blooming cereus that would burst into bloom one evening to the delight of the entire neighborhood. I inherited the cereus and the African violets, but they all promptly died. On the other side of the coin, I had a lot of other types of houseplants that my mother simply could not grow. The bottom line was our differing concepts about watering plants: I overwatered, while she underwatered.

My mother loved visiting other people's gardens. One of the highlights of her life was joining me on a tour of English gardens in the 1980s, where she oohed and aahed over the magical blue poppies, delphiniums, and lupins that seemed to grow everywhere. One time, when I was living in England, she had me bring back seed for the blue poppies, but after trying her darnedest to get them to germinate, they simply didn't work. By this time, Louise had given up lampshade-making and the like and taken up more genteel pursuits, such as needlepoint. One of her treasures was a petitpoint bridge table cover, filled with blue poppies, delphiniums, and lupins, that was especially designed for her by the Royal School of Needlework. It took her nearly thirty years to complete, by which time she was no longer playing bridge and had to work with magnifying glasses.

Louise could be a sharp critic of other people's gardens. After my husband and I moved to the Boston area, we hired two women to design my front garden, since I was getting nowhere on my own and deeply involved in running a full-time business. They suggested all sorts of plants, some of which I didn't like that well, but for the most part I put them in. One of the glories of my garden is the array of large-leaved hostas, now considered "structure" plants. I was somewhat nervous when my mother came for a visit shortly after the garden was installed, but was hoping she'd give it her stamp of approval. She took one look at the hostas and said, "Why don't you get rid of those awful funkias?" (the old name for hostas). I was crushed, but in thinking about it I remembered in a flash why she didn't like them. When we lived in Brightwaters, she had an unforgiving double line of "funkias" lining the driveway. They were small leaved and variegated to boot and hard to kill. She must have hated them with a passion.

I'd like to say that my mother mellowed in old age, but she didn't. Her outspokenness, wicked sense of humor, and boundless energy endeared her to me all the more as I grew older and wiser. She never could understand why someone (namely my father) would want to loll about in bed on a fine morning when there was so much one could do, such as going into New York City for the day or pottering in the garden. Just before my mother died at age eighty, she asked that I scatter her ashes in her favorite garden in England, at Harrogate, where she had first seen the blue poppies. I complied, bringing along a small bag of her ashes in my pocketbook. This was long before the days of airport security screenings where a plastic bag filled with a grainy white substance would have been regarded with the utmost suspicion. Every now and then I return to Harrogate to have a quick visit with Louise, knowing that she is happy resting among her favorite plants.

CHAPTER 14

"Mother's Day Visit"

by Briggs Nisbet

My mother's garden is nearing its half century. She has been tending it for most of those years. I remember when we moved into the house how large and exotic the yard seemed. Someone, probably the original owners, had carefully planned the two large patios, and laid out the paths from the side yard to the back. They had also planted things oddly out of place in this western landscape—a huge evergreen magnolia tree, a lilac bush, camellias, an apple tree, and a concord grape on a metal arbor. Also, a weeping cherry, an elm, and a mimosa or silk tree. Only the magnolia and the silk tree remain.

It all had a rather Southern feel to me. I think less because I knew what a Southern garden looked like than because of the paper mural that covered a wall of the living room of the house. My mother loved that wallpaper. But then, she is a Southern girl at heart. The mural was a source of embarrassment and even shame for me although I liked having a picture of a vast garden on our wall. However, the gray-green groves of rhododendron and palmettos and weeping willow trees by a meandering river couldn't make up for the looming white mansion with its columned portico. It probably wasn't Tara itself. But it might as well have been. A wallpaper plantation was a suspicious oddity in this suburb of middle class "ranches" and fifties-style tract homes in the post–civil rights era.

The plantation is still on the wall but the garden has changed dramatically. It no longer looks Southern at all. The trees and shrubbery are not contained in their plots and have lost the shape they were put there to display. It's as if they have outgrown their gardener, found their own character and defied the design they had no part in planning.

Mother's roses are old, the canes gray. Her Victorian "knot" garden of clipped herbs now is more of a labyrinth, with bare spots in the hedges. My father's lawn is weary. He tells me he's through with trying to keep it green and wants to cover it with redwood bark. And the silk tree is dying.

It used to shade half the garden with its far-reaching limbs of feathery green. Like great green wings, its boughs seemed to float above the patio, quelling the dry heat and bringing a deep and pleasant shade.

I stood under it today and could see mostly sky through its remaining branches, gradually lopped off as the rot claimed them. My mother said the tree man told her it had maybe a few more years before it would have to be taken out. She talked about planting a new tree near the old one, to start it before the silk tree died. But they haven't done that yet. And I am not sure they will.

CHAPTER 15

FROM *Cultivating Delight*

by Diane Ackerman

Bill phoned early yesterday morning to say that he and Chrys had an emergency and would come a day later to help bind up the leaf doilies. When they arrived this morning, Chrys looked troubled. She explained that a client of hers, an older woman whose garden they had planted many years ago and continue to maintain, telephoned in some distress. The lady was moving to Florida in three weeks and she had given her home to her son and daughter-in-law and their new baby. The young couple had decided that they didn't want a garden but a nice flat lawn for their child to run around on. So they phoned a landscape company and instructed it to tear out the entire garden—flowers, paving stones, ornamentals, everything—and just dump it in the woods. Anger welled up in Chrys as she described the face of the woman watching her beloved garden full of memories being destroyed. Chrys of the ponytail, columbine tattoo, and gentle ways. That any son could be so selfish seemed unimaginable.

"He couldn't wait three weeks until his mother left?" she said angrily.

"What on earth did you do?" I asked.

Chrys explained that she and Bill had salvaged the shade-loving plants and settled them in the woods behind the house. The rosebushes and other flowers they loaded into their trunk. Then Chrys had tried to comfort the woman by promising to plant exactly the same garden, adding that whenever she came north she could visit it and see it blooming.

"Imagine," Chrys said in anguish, "he told the landscape company to rip all the flowers out—even the tea roses—and dump them all in a trash pile in the woods. He did this while his mother watched!"

Why not drive a knife into her heart? It was worse than putting her out to pasture. It was pure Greek tragedy—a son uprooting the most vital part of his mother's life, the blooming part she had been cultivating for years. Why did he feel the need to destroy her perfectly nurtured little world, one of her last sources of pleasure and accomplishment, her belief in a future she would live to see? Why do so in front of her, if not as an expression of his power? It's hard to guess what revenge drama he might have been staging.

CHAPTER 16

"The Garden in Winter"

from *My Garden (Book)*

by Jamaica Kincaid

One summer, early in the afternoon, I went to visit my friend Love. She and her mother (a perfectly nice woman, just to look at her) were walking in her garden. (Love's garden is in the shape of an enormous circle, subdivided into long and short rectangular-shaped beds, half-circle-shaped beds, square-shaped beds, and it is separated from her house by a wide sheet of obsessively well-cut grass and a deep border of iris, foxglove, and other June/July flower-bearing perennials.) Love was in a fretful mood (her mother's presence had made her that way) and was looking forward to seeing me (she told me so) and feeding me dinner, because I like the food she cooks (and in summer it is almost always something she has grown herself) and also perhaps because my presence would be a relief (this was not said, she did not tell me this). As Love and her mother walked around, they removed faded flowers, plants, and vegetables that were ready to be harvested (because Love grows vegetables and flowers quite freely together) and exchanged the silences and sentences typical of people who are bound together in a way they did not choose and cannot help (and so do not like), when her mother came on the bed where the Asiatic lilies were in bloom and broke one of their exchanges of silence by saying to her, "Just look at these nigger colors." Love was shocked by her mother saying this, but not surprised; after all, this was her mother, whom she had known for a long time.

Not so very long after Love and her mother had been walking in her garden, I arrived, and while Love stayed in the house and made us cocktails and small snacks of vegetables and a dip, her mother and I walked through the garden, because I had asked to do so (I always walk through Love's garden, but it is usually by myself), and her mother and I exchanged monuments of praise to Love's gardening ability, and when we came to the bed of Asiatic lilies, I was visibly listening to Love's mother tell me some not very important piece of gardening information (I cannot remember it now and so that is why I say it was not very important), but to myself I was wondering if, since I did not know her very well and was not very sure if I liked her, I should be my natural and true self or unnatural and untrue with her. Without being conscious of which self I had decided upon, I blurted out something true. I said, pointing to the Asiatic lilies, "I hate these colors." And then I went back to being unnatural and untrue, and would have forgotten that entire afternoon altogether except that after dinner, while Love and I were doing the dishes alone, she vented to me some of the irritation she felt toward the many people in her life whom she loved but did not like. She told me of her mother's casual but hateful remark, and I became so annoyed with myself for not sensing immediately the true nature of the person with whom I had taken a walk in the garden, for had I known, I would have embraced the Asiatic lilies and their repulsive colors with a force that perhaps only death could weaken. If someone will go to such lengths to nourish and cultivate prejudice, extending to an innocent flower the malice heaped on innocent people, then I certainly wouldn't want to be the one to stand between her and her pleasure.

CHAPTER 17

"Seeds for My Mother"

by Linda M. Frank

It began with a seed.

Dwarfed by the ten-foot chain-link fence, dividing our apartment building's backyard from the neighboring brownstone, I stood uneasily near the rambling, blue-flowered vine, which twined its way up and spilled over the other side of the fence. My older brother reached into the twisted mat of stems and plucked off what appeared to be a dried, brown pea and placed it in the palm of my small hand.

I was five years old and already accustomed to this typical

twelve-year-old boy's teasing of his little sister. So when he urged, "Go ahead. Don't be afraid. Just squeeze the pod and see what's inside," I was justifiably skeptical. Despite the fact that his smile and enthusiasm did seem genuine, I wasn't about to oblige him quite so easily with yet another opportunity to frighten me.

"There'd better not be a bug in there!" I warned him. But, to ensure my safety, I dug in my heels and enlisted the ultimate threat. "If it IS a bug, I'm gonna tell Mommy on you!" Usually this was when he'd weigh the possible punishment from my mother versus the adolescent satisfaction of having successfully pulled off another little-sister coup.

But, now he showed no concern or hesitation when I cautioned him with my intent. He was almost . . . sincere. Even more strange to me than his behavior was the disquieting reality of where we were standing at that very moment. More specifically, where I was standing. Where I was allowed to be standing. My brother had never before permitted me to step foot in his garden domain. Admittedly, I was at that age when I could have thoughtlessly wandered off the pathways he'd so painstakingly delineated by wooden stakes and twine and plunged my Mary Janes into his bed of radishes or zinnias. So, why, now was he being so gracious?

At eleven years old, he had carved out a little garden oasis in the backyard of our three-story apartment building in Brooklyn, New York. He cleared away bricks, bits of concrete, ground ivy, dandelions, old shoes, and even a tire or two. He also tackled the daunting task of hacking through and digging out each and every one of the native trees of Brooklyn: The Stinkweed Tree. For years, the tall, noxious weed tree dominated the yard, creating an inhospitable, canopied jungle. To touch it, brush up against it, or venture within a two-foot radius of the plant left a stench on your clothes and skin and haunted your nasal passages throughout the day. People in the neighborhood could easily tell where you'd been and gave you a pretty wide berth as you passed. Several hot baths, contaminated clothes washed two or three times in my mother's old barrel-shaped wringer-washer, and patience till the smell left your nostrils were the only curatives to treat the lingering odor. We could never understand why the landlord erected a fence between the backyards in the first place. What was there to protect? Who'd want to go in there anyway? Even city pigeons; with their thug-like stamina to roost in garbage heaps, couldn't seem to wing their way fast enough over back lots peppered with *Ailanthus altissima*.

Yep. *Ailanthus altissima*. Pretty fancy-shmancy, high falutin name for a plant so insidious and offensive. Incredibly, it's also known as "The Tree of Heaven." Yet again, dubiously distinguished by another name: "The Tree That Grew in Brooklyn." While its sheer proliferation throughout the borough could easily explain that title, it's more likely attributable to its folkloric association with the proverbial "Tree" of the Betty Smith novel and the 1945 movie of a similar name.

Growing upwards of twenty feet, producing an umbrella of fan-like, ferny leaves atop bare, spindly trunks, ailanthus would bully any interloping weed into submission. Dominating nearly every vacant lot and backyard just like ours. Despite its "stinky" reputation, and since I've always been fascinated with a plant's origin, I found its historical arrival and growth in this country rather noteworthy.

A native plant of China, ailanthus trees produce abundant and extremely lightweight seeds. In the 1800s, these seeds were used as packing material in dishes imported from China to New York. This "packing material" was ultimately dispensed as railroad ballast to line railbeds from New York to Boston. Hitching rides on locomotive wheels, the weightless seeds would be carried all along the Northeast corridor, germinating and surviving in the most unlikely and harsh environments. While female plants can be quite beautiful and odorless, the male tree is the smelly culprit emitting the vile and putrid odor. Obviously, it was the more viable male seeds that survived their rail journey over a century ago and had taken up residence in our backyard, eventually to become my brother's foe.

Each day after school my brother, Don, trudged down the steps to the basement of our century-old brownstone. A dark, musty, and foreboding place, the cellar was lit by only one single bulb dangling from a chain. He'd pass locked storage bins and ominous nooks and crannies echoing with strange clanking noises from enormous sewage pipes and creaking timbers. Only to face the most most feared of all obstacles . . . The Furnace. A behemoth of belching coal smoke, it radiated such tremendous heat that it could singe your dungarees if you slid within a yard of it. The golden-red flames sputtering behind the cast-iron grill portrayed a devilishly grinning, frightening face. Needless to say, it took a mighty amount of courage and dedication for any kid under twelve (and some grown-ups) to precariously maneuver around that roaring, rumbling monster each day. But, always, Don kept one eye on the beast and the other focused beyond the shadows toward the dappled daylight streaming through milky glass windowpanes of the backyard door.

I don't remember how long it took him to create his garden. I was only three or four when he began, and I imagine the most important thing on my mind then was whether or not to outline the drawings in my coloring book. (I always outlined.

No doubt, a precursor to my present-day anal attention to perfectly edged flower beds and a covetous attachment to my half-moon edger.)

Don's determination to clear the yard and create his garden began with a package of morning glory seeds from my mother. Planting those seeds at the base of the chain-link fence, which protected the neighbors from the our stinkweed invasion and watching them grow and flower, was all the incentive he needed. After wading through the odious weeds which towered over his head, he initially just managed to clean and scratch out a piece of ground near the fence to plant the future vines. He'd haul down a pail of water every day or so from our second-floor apartment to help the seedlings along as they twined higher toward the sun through another link in the chain-link fence despite the onslaught of shadowy weeds. As the vine grew, so did his excitement. And with the sight of that first, heavenly blue flower, he was hooked. His garden quest had begun, and the stinkweed trees would become history.

A year later, I had finally been invited into his path-lined sanctuary and held in my cupped hand what I would learn was the seedpod of one of those beautiful blue blooms. It was time to start my journey. My quest. My initiation into gardening. At that precise moment, however, standing in the middle of Don's hallowed garden, my only thoughts were of self-preservation. Just how fast could I escape without tripping over the pathway markers, when that bug or worm crept out of that brown pea? Could I brave running past the fearsome furnace or just scream as loud as I could, hoping my cries would be heard by my mother in the kitchen upstairs?

But, Don was still so insistent and earnest. "I swear, Linda, it's not gonna be bad. There's nothing in there that'll hurt you. I swear on Brownie."

Now, I should tell you that there were certain things in my family that were sacrosanct. And using the name of Brownie, our beautiful, beloved cocker spaniel, to further any of Don's little-sister-teasing tricks was just . . . well, just unthinkable.

Still apprehensive, but a bit more encouraged by his pledge on Brownie, I whispered, "Okay. 'Long as you said Brownie."

Holding the pod over the palm of my other hand and gently squeezing it between my thumb and index finger, out fell two, hard, black seeds. Roundish on one side and slightly concave on the other. When my heart finally stopped pounding in my ears, I realized there wasn't any reason to run. Quite the opposite. I was . . . a bit mesmerized, staring at these two completely innocent little black pebbles in my hand.

"See. I told you it'd be okay," Don affirmed. Prompted by my obvious intrigue, he pursued, "Do you know what those are?"

I didn't of course, but I did know he took that brown pea thing off the blue-flowered vines on the fence.

He pointed up toward the vine. "See those blue flowers up there?"

I was drawn into his words like the bees plunging their heads into the throats of those very blossoms. I stared at him now. A captive audience, I held on his every word.

"This thing growing up the fence. It's called a morning glory vine, and those flowers are called morning glory flowers 'cause they open up in the morning, and they're closed when you get home from school."

He was eager to share what he knew (just like a gardener) and continued in words a five-year-old would understand. "Well, when the flower closes up at the end of the day and goes away, that brown pod thing starts to grow in its place and inside it are those black things. They're called seeds."

I never knew my brother was so smart. He suddenly seemed a lot older to me. Wiser. He knew about these things. I felt special. Privileged that he was sharing this with his little sister.

He knelt down on the ground near the fence and asked, "Do you know what you can do with those seeds you've got there in your hand?"

I shook my head back and forth. "Nuh-uh."

"Kneel down here with me." This was too much. I was overwhelmed. Or as overwhelmed as a five-year-old could be. He was actually asking me to kneel down in his garden soil!

Momentarily taking the seeds from my hand, he gestured

toward the ground. "If you hold on to these seeds till next year, in the springtime, you can come back down to the garden and put them right here. In the ground. Then a few months later in the summer, before you go back to school, you'll get more of those pretty blue flowers."

Zounds! I could feel the gardening tendrils winding their way around my ankles, working their way up my torso like the morning glory vine up the fence, ultimately rooting in my heart, where they'd bloom for the rest of my life.

I did as Don instructed and saved the morning glory seeds. I kept them in a sealed, pink envelope of my mother's stationery which bore the big block letters: SEEDS. Throughout the winter, the envelope remained prominently displayed on my bureau dresser. Each morning before heading off to school, I'd pick it up, running my fingers over the outline of the seeds inside and wonder how much longer it would be till spring.

When next spring finally came and the soil in his brownstone garden warmed, Don asked me to work alongside him. He allowed me to help him tie the string around some of the stakes to mark the paths. But, my big assignment, the one I was to handle all on my own, was to print the seed markers. In big, block, first-grade letters, I wrote CARROTS, MARIGOLDS, RADISHES, etc. on poster board, and he stapled them to pieces of wood shim. I was also awarded the honor of placing the RADISH seed marker in that part of the garden, which in a month or so would produce those little red globes. I felt I was becoming a part of my brother's garden. No longer relegated to viewing from the cellar door or our second-floor kitchen window. I had found a whole new world to explore. To learn about. To enjoy. To dream of growing things and seeds and big blue flowers.

I was eager, now, to open the envelope. To retrieve the seeds from last year. To plant them. My seeds. To grow my very own flowers. Each day I pestered my brother, "Is it time yet? Can I plant them now? How much longer do we have to wait? Is it warm enough?" Till, mercifully, he pronounced the ground ready. He no longer thought the weather would turn cold enough to harm the seeds. It was the day before Mother's Day when he asked me to get the pink envelope. I could have planted them that day, but despite all my prior eagerness, I now wanted to wait till Sunday. Mother's Day. I told him I wanted to plant them as a present for Mommy.

To a child, a day can seem an eternity, and the germination of those seeds seemed to take forever. In fact it only took four days from that Mother's Day morning to Thursday when the pods poked through the soil. By Saturday, they'd grown two inches. The spindly stems barely able to support the nodding pods. After Sunday breakfast, my brother took me down to the garden to see the pod had cracked, revealing tightly bound, green leaves pushing from between the pod's spreading arms.

Within an hour the arms would lie broken on the ground. There seemed to be new developments each day. The stems grew. Then wispy tendrils grew from the stems. Still more tendrils. Every morning. Higher and higher. Till they'd stretched enough to begin their winding journey up and around the fence. But days passed, weeks passed and all I could see on the fence was an ever-spreading green vine waving its heart-shaped leaves. I remember worrying that Don may have mistakenly given me the wrong seeds. Maybe these had been the leaf seeds, I thought. Not the seeds that made the flowers.

By midsummer the vine had climbed nearly eight feet up the ten-foot fence. But I no longer raced with much enthusiasm to the kitchen window. No longer squinted, with anticipation, through the balcony railing to see a hint of blue. I tried to hide my disappointment from my mother. But she knew. She tried encouraging me to have just a bit more patience and I'd be rewarded. Patience is a hard virtue to come by in a child. It was near nonexistent in me. So, I'd given up any hope of ever seeing my mother's flowers.

Until one morning in mid-August. Dragging myself to the kitchen window, my first thoughts those mornings were of school recess ending in three weeks. Second grade. There were definitely more important things to think about now. More important than even those blue flowers. But would I ever really get over my disappointment of not being able to grow my mother's flowers? Would I ever have the courage to try growing flowers for her again?

As the first shafts of sunlight slid across the brick walls of the clustered apartment buildings, bathing my brother's garden and the chain-link fence in its nurturing warmth, I reluctantly pulled back the kitchen curtains and looked down. And there it was. Even from our second-floor apartment, I could see it. Huge. At least four inches across. Clear blue with a white throat. Its face smiling toward the sun. It was my Mother's morning glory. I was stunned. Amazed and relieved. I didn't know whether to run down there and admire it up close or call my mother to the window to come and see her flower. The flower I grew for her from those wondrous seeds. My mind raced. Thinking ahead to the following year. (Typical gardener.) Next spring I'd again grow her blue flowers along the fence. Maybe my brother would let me plant the marigold seeds, too. Maybe he would even give me a special place in his garden where I could grow all sorts of flowers for my mother. A spot I could mark off with string and stakes and place my own block-printed sign on a piece of shim. "MOMMY'S FLOWERS" it would read. Maybe . . . maybe one day I'd even have my very own garden, and every year I'd grow the morning glories there just for her. I'd grow flowers and vegetables. Birds would come and butterflies, and I'd have her sit on a bench and just drink it all in. She would love that and so would I.

All the dreams. All that envisioned beauty. All the things I wanted to learn. I wanted to share it all with her. All because of those tiny, brown seeds from my brother's garden. Seeds that grew my mother's morning glories. Seeds which also grew the gardener within me.

These days, seeds seem smaller in my grown-up hand. I'm still amazed at the bountiful beauty held inside each tiny speck. I'm still impatient to see them bloom as I scatter them throughout my garden. The garden of my childhood dreams. The garden that my mother would have so loved.

September 15th would have been my mother's eighty-fourth birthday.

Every year I plant blue morning glories in my garden just for her.

CHAPTER 18

"Wasps and Their Ways"

by Margaret W. Morley

STARTING THE NEST

The well-known grey structures wasps build in trees, under the eaves or in the ground, are generally seen in the fall of the year. Then the leaves have left the tree branches bare disclosing the nests so carefully hidden under the foliage in the summer time.

Moreover, in the fall of the year, boys fearlessly take down these nests and hang them up as ornaments in the house.

Boys do not take them down in the summer—for a very good reason; but they know that after the first frost the nest has no fiery occupants to defend it; it is an abandoned domicile—safe booty for whoever finds it.

Sometimes a hornet's nest is nearly as large as a bushel basket, but that is at the end of the season. The beginning of every nest is simple enough, and consists of but a cluster of three small cells.

Early in the summer the females of the social wasp may be seen flying about, searching everywhere for a good building-site.

One is suspicious that Madam Vespa uses this nest-hunting as excuse for a prolonged lark, seizing the opportunity to investigate her little universe, and find out a great many things besides the best location for a home. The large yellow queens of the yellow-jackets may be seen flying about in the spring, peering into every cranny in the woods, investigating every fallen log and heap of rubbish, poising on vibrating wings under the eaves of buildings, examining every growing tree, bush, or herb, and what is more noticeable, examining with equal minuteness any human brother who happens to be abroad. Certainly they do not intend to suspend a nest from any part of your person, yet they favor you with as prolonged and careful an examination as they give to any tree, or rock, or roof.

If the windows are open they are sure to come into the house; then they are in a state of consuming curiosity. What does everything mean? They examine each article of furniture in a comically thorough manner, flying around and behind it, and hanging buzzing so close to it that they seem to be testing its quality with their antennae. Sometimes it is but one or two objects that thus occupy them, sometimes one of them will remain an hour in a room satisfying herself concerning every object in it, not slighting any quiet and inoffensive occupant that may be there. Indeed the human owner of this strange nest seems oftentimes to puzzle her more than all else, and if one but keeps still she proceeds upon a very flattering inspection—very likely poising directly in front of one's eyes, so close that the breeze made by her little wings can be distinctly felt. Her small face is close to yours, her large eyes gazing intently into your own; and there she hangs while you, flattered by her close attention, sit and look calmly back at her or close your eyes until the close buzzing of her ladyship ceases to roar in your ears. One living in a region of wasps becomes quite familiar with these spring visits, and at least one person feels slighted if Queen Vespa enters the room and goes out without noticing its human occupant. It is unnecessary to say that wasps under such circumstances never sting. They are simply about their business, trying to get an education out of the only book at their command. In a few weeks these large yellow queens disappear. Other, smaller, less prodigally yellow creatures roam the fields, but the large queens are absorbed in domestic duties that keep them within their doors.

The queen-hornets also intrude their black-and-white presence in people's houses in the spring, but they do not seem so curious nor so friendly. Their investigations seem rather aimless, in comparison with those of their yellow relative, and their manner is much more suspicious and, if one may say so, tempestuous.

Only the perfect females, or "queens," of the Vespae survive the winter, and when they are wakened to life by the warm sun of early summer, each little queen wasp has upon her shoulders the responsibility of the whole family—she must build her own house as well as take care of her own offspring. She does not start in life, like the queen bee, with thousands of helpers ready to do all the work and even to feed her royal highness.

She must do everything for herself, at least at first.

When she has found a place to her mind, perhaps in the branches of a tree, or under the projecting eaves of a building, or in a hole in the ground, Vespa betakes herself to a grey and weatherworn rail, or to an old stump, and there she sits and gnaws lengthwise of the grain until she has a little bundle of wood-fibre in her jaws.

This she takes to her chosen site and chews into pulp, mixing it with saliva from her mouth.

Now behold the first paper-maker of the world at work!

For the social wasps were making a serviceable paper ages and ages before man dreamed of such a thing.

When the Egyptians were laboriously cutting their records in stone, or drawing them up on the pressed pith of the papyrus, and the Europeans theirs on the inner bark of trees, and the North American Indians were tanning the hides of animals and painting their messages upon them, the wasp folk were busy making a true paper, a paper that man finally learned to make, in essentially the same way that the wasp makes it.

For paper is only vegetable fibre reduced to pulp and pressed into sheets.

Having gathered her little ball of wood-fibre, and reduced it to a pulp of proper consistency by chewing and moistening with sticky saliva, Vespa first builds a slender stem or support for her future home.

To the end of this she hangs a little cluster of three or more hexagonal cells, also of paper.

She begins at the roof and builds down, suspending her habitation from above, instead of building it on foundations that rest on the earth.

She begins her first cell, but does not finish it before she starts another, and when she has a cluster of three half-finished cells she lays an egg in the first one, and goes on building. As fast as the cells are large enough she deposits an oblong white egg in each, placing it in an angle of the cell and about one half or two thirds down, or what will be one half or two thirds down when the cell is finished.

Her cells are six-sided, and are like honey-comb cells, excepting that they are made of paper instead of wax, and are suspended mouth down instead of lying on one side.

Since the cells hang mouth down, one naturally wonders why the eggs do not fall out as soon as put in.

The reason is that each is covered with a sticky substance, so that it is glued firmly to the cell wall.

The ancients had as little idea of the origin of wasps as they had of the origin of bees, and while they believed the bees were bred from the decaying carcass of a bull, the wasps, they tell us, came from the dead body of an ass or a horse, the fierce swift hornets owing their origin to the body of a war-horse.

There was also a superstition among the Egyptians that wasps were generated from the decaying carcass of a crocodile.

However, a later generation discovered that wasps proceed from eggs laid in the cells of the nest by the queen wasp.

The egg is generally placed in an inner angle of the cell, and is attached by one end.

Her first three cells completed, Vespa starts another row of cells around them, depositing an egg in each as soon as it is ready.

She evidently does not consider these exposed cells a safe resting-place for her progeny, for no sooner has she formed a little group of nine or a dozen cells than she proceeds to make a paper wall about them.

The result of her labours is a pretty little grey ball, with a hole in the bottom, enclosing the group of cells, but not attached to them. The first wall made consists of but one layer of grey paper, and at that stage the nest looks its prettiest.

Vespa finally devotes all her time to caring for her progeny, for in a few days the first eggs laid have hatched into tiny white maggot-like larvae, and every day more eggs hatch out. Queen Vespa is obliged to go hunting for food for these ravenous infants. They are still attached to the side of the cell by the tail end, but their mouths are free, and are always ready to open for something to be put in.

They have little round white heads, with little pin points of eyes and a pair of tiny, brown, horny jaws. The eyes of the larva are simple, the compound eyes not appearing until the adult form. When the comb is jarred, out are thrust all these little heads, and the mouths are opened wide, for they suppose that Mother Vespa is coming to feed them.

When a number of the eggs have hatched, Vespa devotes most of her time to catching flies and other insects, chewing them up, and feeding the hungry youngsters in the cells with them.

One is reminded of a mother bird feeding her nestlings, when watching the mother wasp going from cell to cell, and putting food into each little open mouth.

The larvae are always ready to open their mouths, and it is no wonder they are forever asking for more, as they grow at a marvellous rate, in the course of a few days filling their cradle cells with their plump, white bodies.

One trying ordeal every young Vespa has to pass through, and that is the change of position in its downward-opening cell. Since the egg is glued to an angle of the cell part way down, when it hatches, the larva grasps the cell with two little feet at the end of its tail, at the same spot where it was hatched. As it grows larger, however, it must manage somehow to reach the bottom of the cell, so that it may have room to continue its growth.

This migration to the bottom of the cell necessitates turning around twice, letting go its hold on the side of the cell, and yet keeping its position in the downward-pointing cell so as not to fall out.

If the difficult feat of letting go, turning around, and moving to the bottom of the cell is accomplished, all is well.

But sometimes it is not accomplished. Poor baby Vespa,

using her still useful tail-feet and her jaws to hang on by, slips or makes a miscalculation, and out it tumbles head over heels.

It is said the mother wasp sometimes puts it back after such an accident but generally it lies and wriggles in the cold outer world until death claims it.

Or if it falls out later in the season the worker wasps carry it out of the nest and leave it to perish.

But if it once gets fixed in the bottom of the cell, with its head hanging down, all it has to do is to stay there.

This may look difficult, but it is really easy, for young Vespa is now a fat, white grub, or larva, with a brown head, footless, it is true, but with a way of ruffling up the sides of its body that enables it to fit tightly in the cell and there remain.

When the larva has reached the limit of its growth it finds its mouth full of silk. This comes out through a hole in its lip, and whenever it touches anything with its mouth little viscid threads like saliva are drawn out, and these harden into a fine, glistening silk.

Now young Vespa ceases to crave food. She touches the side of her cell with her mouth, draws back her head, touches another part of her cell, draws back her head—each time pulling out sticky threads that harden into silk.

Thus moving her head about, she lines all but the bottom

of her cell with soft, tough, white silk; then she reaches out her head and weaves back and forth, back and forth, over the opening to her cell, until she has formed a strong cap or roof over her head. From the very beginning she has more responsibility than the young bee; no fond nurse seals the opening to her cell, she is obliged to do that wholly for herself. The cap made, the infant is now lying in a silken bag of her own manufacture, open at one end and closed at the other with a cap of silk that is heavier than the silk used in making the rest of the bag.

Her cocoon, if such it can be called, is much heavier and stronger than the similar covering the young bee makes for itself.

She is now safely wrapped up, her silk covering preventing the too rapid evaporation of the juices of her body.

Lying there motionless, a marvellous change comes over her. She loses her fat larval form, a waist line appears, below it is a ringed abdomen, above it is a thorax with incipient legs and wings, and a waspish-looking head.

She is now a "pupa," and at one stage of her transformation is a very charming little creature, as she is as white as snow, and has the daintiest legs and antennae lying close to her body.

As time goes on, however, she grows darker-coloured until finally a perfect wasp lies in the silk-lined cell.

* * *

During her larval life Vespa sheds her skin as she increases in size, and finally, throwing off the last delicate covering from her pupal body, she is ready to step forth into the world and see what is going on there.

She reaches out her jaws, which are much larger and stronger than the brown dots of jaws she possessed as a larva, and with them cuts a hole in the cap she spun over her head a few days ago. As she works she moistens the spot with saliva.

Snip, snip, snip, go the jaws in the dark cell.

One can easily hear them at work. Then a little opening appears. Snip, snip, snip, go the jaws until the hole is large enough to let out one of the antennae.

This organ, newly freed from confinement, waves about as though examining the world into which its little owner is about to enter.

But the jaws are still snipping, and finally the cap is so nearly cut away that Vespa's face can be seen filling the opening of the cell.

Then a foot appears, a fore-leg is stretched out, and very likely the first thing it does is to clean the antenna.

It is very amusing to watch a young Vespa coming out of its cell, tucked away, all but the head and fore-legs, and industriously cleaning its face and hands and polishing up its antennae.

It takes its time, and when it has rested from the effort of uncapping its cell, and has thoroughly made the toilet of its head and hands, it begins to pull itself out.

It grasps the surrounding comb with its fore-feet, and struggles until it has pulled out its second pair of legs.

The remainder is easy, and in a moment more a shining young wasp stands on the comb and surveys its surroundings.

CHAPTER 19

"My Grandmother's Aprons"

by Patricia Lanza

While touring an Amish Village in Iowa I was drawn to a window display in a sewing store. Wood hangers held a row of bright-colored, bias-tape-trimmed, cotton aprons. The aprons were made from an old pattern, one I was very familiar with.

As I stood on the sidewalk admiring the aprons I remembered my grandmother, Della, and the many aprons she had worn. The popular pattern was from the 1930s and had been featured in women's magazines. Della made her pattern from an apron she found at the rag store and bought for a dime. She would have laughed at the tourist price ($45) of these aprons and scoffed at the lack of quality in the workmanship.

As for me, I just enjoyed the memories the aprons conjured up of a time, a place, and a woman that helped shape and direct my life.

The year was 1935, toward the end of the Depression, and in a modest farmhouse in East Tennessee a young woman gave birth to her first child. The woman was seventeen-year-old Mamie and the baby was a little girl. It was Della's house, Mamie was her daughter, and I was the baby. The labor was quick and, as soon as I made my entrance, Dr. Dooley handed me to my grandmother and she wrapped me in her apron.

At that time aprons were mostly worn to protect a woman's dress but they were so much more. They acted as pot holders; the ends of the apron folded up, to take a hot pan off the stove or out of the oven. They substituted for baskets; the bottom ends caught up in one hand creating a pouch, used to carry fresh picked vegetables from the garden and pea hulls and apple peelings to the compost pile. And once-in-a-lifetime holding a newborn grandchild.

Each day when Della went to the henhouse she carried chicken feed in her apron to scatter and then carried fresh eggs back to the kitchen. Her apron pockets were filled with clothespins as she carried wet clothes to hang on the line and the pockets filled with pins again when she removed the dry clothes.

Aprons were a handy substitute for a cloth that could do any of the hundreds of everyday tasks from polishing an apple to polishing silverware. Women wiped steam from their glasses, wiped a spot in the frosted window to see out, and constantly used to wipe their hands.

Times were hard everywhere during the Depression and it was common for families to travel from their homes to find work. When I was about three years old my parents moved to Detroit, Michigan, to work in the factories. They left me behind with my grandmother.

With her children grown and gone Della lived alone. She enjoyed the solitude and well-deserved peace and quiet. Everything changed for her when I moved in and, as I look back, I wonder at her easy acceptance of the changes.

Since she was a small child Della had been in charge of her family. She was removed from school during the third grade when her mother, Sarah, became ill. With four younger siblings and an invalid mother to care for Della, at age ten, was required to do the work of an adult.

Instead of school, young Della learned homemaking; cooking, cleaning, gardening, sewing, and food preparation and preserving. She learned to wash and iron clothes, make quilts, and hook rugs. By the time she was a teen she could shoot small game or wring the neck of a chicken, clean and cook it, and have it on the table for dinner. She chopped wood, carried water, and could repair the roof when needed.

Della learned the importance of raising part of the family's food; chickens, pigs, and keeping a milk cow. These lessons, learned when she was just a small child and honed through the years, helped her live a good, rich life in a poor, austere time and place.

At age forty-two Della became a grandmother. She was still strong and just three years later, in 1938, took on the full-time care of a three-year-old. Her solitary lifestyle disappeared and as her life changed she included me in her daily routine.

Spring rituals had always included the arrival of 100 baby chicks by mail. They were delivered to Della's rural mailbox and after retrieving the box Della would place the 100 bundles of peeping, yellow fluff in a large wooden crate behind the wood stove. The baby chicks stayed warm in the protected environment and their food and water could be monitored frequently.

When it was time to move the chicks to a larger box, or outside to the chicken house, Della would pull up the corners of her apron, scoop up several chicks into the makeshift pouch, and carry them to their new home. When I cried over the death of a baby chick she wiped my tears with her apron.

Grandmother had a collection of aprons. There were a few good aprons, made from nice materials, worn for company and special occasions. Her everyday aprons, made from feed or flour sacks or remnants of old clothing, were worn indoors. Her work aprons, made from fabrics that had begun life as homespun or as heavy feed sacks, comprised the bulk of the collection.

These sturdy work aprons were made to cover her whole dress, from chest to hem. They were worn for dirty, outside work, including gardening, boiling clothes, care and feeding of farm animals, maintenance of farm buildings, and soap making.

There was a great, black, iron pot that sat permanently in the yard near the back porch. It was used for jobs too big for the kitchen. Regardless of the chore Della first had to build a fire to heat water for washing clothes or to render pig fat to make soap. Della's sturdy work apron was used to carry kindling and firewood.

Della's workday began with choosing an apron. She cooked breakfast wearing an indoor-apron that hung on one of the hooks next to the kitchen sink. When she finished with breakfast and housework she stopped at the hook and changed aprons. There was always a clean apron on the hook in case unexpected company came.

Della was a widow who had raised four children supporting

them with a small pension from the railroad and with money earned doing washing, ironing, and sharecropping for her neighbors. She was also a woman of few words. Even as a small child I knew instinctually not to bother her with too many questions. Instead I watched as she changed aprons and shoes that told me what she would be doing that day.

Typical of country women of her day, Della wore dresses, rayon stockings held up with elastic garters, and black leather, lace-up shoes with two-inch fat heels. When her good black shoes were nearly worn out they were recycled as garden shoes. The old shoes sat in a box near the back door where she could step into them on the way outside.

Getting the garden ready each spring was special. After donning her garden apron and old shoes she would bring the mule from the barn (after putting me in a chair on the porch and telling me to stay put), then go to the edge of the garden to hitch the mule to the plow.

I watched from the porch as she lifted the heavy, iron plow with its wooden handles. She would throw the reins over her own slender shoulders and begin to guide the plow up and down the garden. With each pass made with the plow neat furrows of earth peeled back and fat earthworms wiggled to the surface. Della plodded along behind the mule, calling out to him and keeping the plow going in straight rows.

When she finished plowing a row or two she would stop to

rest and, picking up the corner of her apron, use it to wipe the sweat from her face. I watched from my perch on the porch. Years later my grandmother's face would come to my mind as I stopped working in my garden to wipe the sweat from my own face with the corner of my apron.

There was a deep well with sweet-tasting water by the back porch of Della's house. We drew our water from the well by dropping a bucket attached to a rope down into the water. We waited until the bucket filled, then, using the rope, pulled it to the surface.

I learned early I could climb onto a small, wood stool to reach the dipper that hung on a porch rail and bring my grandmother a drink of water. She would take the dipper, drink from it, and swear she never tasted anything as sweet. I would take a drink from the same dipper, spilling the water down my chin, and dry myself on my grandmother's apron.

Garden preparation was a two-day job. Once the garden was plowed it had to be disked then hoed into rows. When the rows were made it was time to plant. Grandmother taught me to count by counting seeds, counting rows, and counting holes made for cabbage and tomato plants.

Grandmother carried the vegetable seeds in her apron pockets. I longed to wear an apron with pockets. My first apron was one of my grandmother's old ones. She would roll it up and tie it under my arms so I wouldn't trip on it. She would fill my pockets with seeds and I would help her plant. I can hear her laughter as she would find a bean plant growing in the corn row or a cucumber growing in among the tomatoes. She would say they had gotten lost from the other seeds of their kind.

One of my sweetest memories is of squatting beside my grandmother in the garden. She once took my hands and showed me how to press the air out of the soil surrounding a plant and how to make a depression around a new plant to catch and hold water.

Leaving me with my grandmother was the best gift my parents ever gave me. We got up with the sun and just before dark quit for the day. The work never ended until we washed up supper dishes. Afterwards we sat in the living room listening to the radio and reading.

My mouth salivates when I think of my grandmother's cooking: fried chicken; pork chops; cornbread; biscuits; hand-churned, cold buttermilk; homemade butter; and thick-sweet-fruit jams. In the summer, as soon as the garden began producing, we would make pouches of our aprons and carry in fresh green beans, cucumbers, and tomatoes. When corn came in we pulled an apronful every day.

The garden provided fresh food for the family during the summer. It was also preserved to keep us in vegetables during the winter. Grandmother preserved by canning, drying, and salting food to fill the pantry shelves.

An apron became an extension of the woman wearing it. I watched as my grandmother rolled her apron into a ball when she was agitated or folded her arms under it to hide her negative body language. I've even seen her pull the apron over her head to muffle her laughter.

As soon as I was old enough to climb the apple tree that grew in the front yard I watched my grandmother work from a distance. She liked to do things alone and I left her alone. It was there in my perch on a limb that I learned most about her daily habits and garden work. It was also from my elevated view I waited for my great-grandfather, Jesse Wyatt, to come down the road.

Every Saturday I watched as his mule topped the hill. I would call out to my grandmother to say he was coming. Jesse sat on a buckboard seat in the open wagon. He would stop the mule at Grandmother's gate, hitched the reins to a fence post, then stand outside the fence with his hat in his hands.

My grandmother would come from the house and stand on her side of the fence with her arms crossed under her apron. They would talk for a short while and then she would turn and walk back to the house. Jesse would put on his hat, get in the wagon, and drive away.

In my entire life I never spoke once to my great-grandfather. Those arms folded under her apron told me my grandmother wouldn't like it. When I wanted to talk about him I was told she was angry with him about choosing the wrong husband for her. Eventually I stopped asking; however, I never stopped watching for him on Saturday.

Winters in Tennessee were not long but we did have snow and the temperatures dropped below freezing often. We spent the winter inside but my grandmother was not idle. She made quilts from old clothes and rugs from sweaters she got from the rag store.

Della's quilts were made mostly to keep us warm but they were also beautiful. She used pieces of old clothes we could identify years later as favorite dresses or shirts. When a quilt top was pieced and ready to be quilted she lowered a frame that hung near the ceiling when not in use. The frame sat on four chair backs and to work my grandmother moved her own chair around the outside of the frame. Her apron's pockets were filled with spools of thread, a thimble, and a little pair of scissors.

Della's hooked rugs were works of art. She drew patterns freehand using a piece of charcoal on the back of burlap bags. For wool she bought boxes of wool sweaters from the rag store. The sweaters were each taken apart, the wool unraveled then rolled into balls. The balls were sorted according to color and stacked in boxes turned on their sides so the colors could be seen and easily accessed.

Grandmother would fill her apron pockets with the balls of yarn then, following the pattern she had drawn, hook the yarn into rugs, using the wool like an artist using oils. Her finished rugs depicted her gardens in summer.

It wasn't the vegetables she drew and preserved in wool but the flowers. Her flower gardens were planted each year with seeds saved from the year before. At the end of the harvest I would watch as my grandmother pulled the bottom of her apron up to make a carrying pouch and begin to harvest dried flower seeds by pulling them from the plant and dropping them into her apron.

Grandmother's flower gardens framed the vegetable garden and were lovingly planted after the hard work of the main garden was finished. When a lesser woman would have stopped working she would prepare a two-foot border around the parameter of the big garden, fill her apron with seeds saved from last year's garden, and plant.

When the seeds bloomed they created a colorful border that lured bees and butterflies. They also provided cut flowers for the house and inspiration for my grandmother's rugs. Flowers I remembered best were larkspur, bachelor buttons, zinnia, cosmos, cleome, marigolds, and nasturtiums.

What child can know what lessons learned from their grandparents will mean in their own lives? I certainly didn't realize how much my grandmother would influence my life. I married young and began my family when most women my age were still in school.

Those first years of married life were pitiful attempts at being a grown-up. For inspiration and guidance I called on memories of my grandmother; how she ran her house and made her gardens. However, those memories were made when I was a small child, sitting on the sidelines of my grandmother's life, and what I remembered were vignettes, not the whole picture.

When I left my grandmother's house for the last time I saved one of her aprons. I often wore it and while washing and ironing it one day I noticed a small tear. I put the apron away but before I did I made a paper pattern. Over the years I used the pattern to make lots of aprons.

After a lifetime of marriage and raising children I moved to a small farm in upstate New York, alone. It was an uncertain time financially but I had a small farm and could try to make my living from the land. After years of wearing many different aprons of my own I donned a canvas garden apron, one with pockets for tools and seeds. I began to turn my hayfields into perennial and herb gardens.

Call me crazy but I began to feel the presence of my grandmother and knew somehow she was still looking out for me. While working in my roadside gardens very good things began to happen; I discovered what I called Lasagna Gardening. This easy method enabled me to make wonderful gardens quickly without extra help.

You've heard of things that stop traffic? My gardens actually did.

One day a woman stopped and asked if she could bring her garden club to my gardens and would I give a talk on my methods. Seventy-five women came.

One day a woman who owned a newspaper stopped by the gardens and asked me to write a weekly column for her paper. After eight years I compiled some of my columns for my first book.

Another day a woman stopped by the gardens and asked me to join a writer's group. I sent in my dues and attended my first meeting a month later. At one of those meetings I met an editor who took my Lasagna Gardening ideas to the publisher who gave me a book contract. Over the next eight years I wrote three books for that company.

One day a man stopped by the gardens and asked if I would like to host a radio talk show, another day a woman stopped and asked if she could bring a tour bus from the Brooklyn Botanic Gardens, and a man stopped and filmed me giving a tour. A few years later I would give the tour on HGTV.

One day at a yearly meeting of my writer's group I met a woman who offered me a job speaking at her home and garden show. That winter I left New York and flew to Florida, where I gave my first talk in an open forum. It was there I met a couple who invited me to be a guest speaker at Epcot.

Over the next twelve years lots of good things happened to me and they began in my gardens. My grandmother's teachings of long ago had fallen on fertile ground and over all the years of my life I used those lessons well.

CHAPTER 20

"A Time of Renewal"

from A Garden's Grace

by Nancy Hutchens

In the morning the sun rose brilliant and quickly melted the thin ice off the water, and the warm air around vibrated with the vapour given off by the awakening earth. Last year's grass grew green again and the young grass thrust up its tiny blades; the buds swelled on the guilder-rose and the currant-bushes . . . Spring had really come.
—Leo Tostoi, *Anna Karenina*

In gardening I've discovered a language that rekindles the joy of my childhood on the farm. Each spring when I was growing up Daddy knew the moment when nature had worked her magic and the ground was ready for planting. Life on the farm was guided by the rhythms of the seasons. Like our ancestors before us, we grew our own food for the body and flowers for the soul. Mother loved her deep pink peonies, tall blue-bearded irises, lilacs, and wild roses; and Daddy always planted sunflowers, zinnias, snapdragons, and morning glories in the kitchen garden. Both of my parents were keeping pace with Mother Nature, so it was my grandmother, Mamaw Tribby, who taught me most about gardening in the hours we spent tending her flowers. While we weeded and watered her beloved yellow roses, she talked about her flowers as if they were her truest, most faithful friends. She believed that gardening was not a hobby but an essential activity that renews the soul as surely as spring renews the earth.

I didn't have my own garden until I was almost thirty, but with every passing year it captures more of my heart. Despite many years of living in cities and suburbs, I've turned into a farmer, just like my Daddy, my grandfathers, and their fathers before them. As I cultivate my own piece of earth dressed in old rubber boots and a threadbare flannel jacket, farming and gardening seem to be a part of the same ancient process of clearing the land, preparing the soil, and planting our sustenance. At work in my flower beds, I'm often surprised by tiny sensory impressions that summon memories of home and a way of life I left long ago. The vivid smells of springtime—pungent composted manure and sweet hyacinths—and sights like a field of yellow daffodils evoke those years with a clarity that words cannot express. When I clear out the soggy leaves that cradle my early daffodils, I can almost hear my Mamaw Tribby saying, "One of these days you'll move away from the farm, but in the spring when the daffodils return and the earth is young again you'll recall these times." She died many years ago, but when I'm in the garden her voice is still there by my side offering down-to-earth advice and reminding me of the simple happiness I've always found there.

CHAPTER 21

"The Need for Solitude, Stillness, and Reflection"

from *The Sanctuary Garden*

by Christopher Forrest McDowell and Tricia Clark-McDowell

The soul has an inherent need for balance. Compelled to *do*, it desires worldly immersion and enchantment, but the soul also needs to know it can just *be*. This *being* means occasional retreat from the frontlines of life—retreat into solitude, stillness, and reflection.

A Sanctuary Garden allows both doing and being to find

natural balance in its Keeper. However, the design of a Sanctuary Garden especially incorporates opportunities to just *be*. Special sitting areas are important. So are meandering paths. Central landscape features such as a waterfall, pond, tree, or rock formation are each important in drawing a visitor to sit quietly in observation. Lastly, a hidden room or nook in the garden is perfect for soliciting solitude and reflection.

What is it like to just *be?* In *Sisters of the Earth*, a collection of women's prose and poetry about Nature, editor Lorraine Anderson talks about "making a conscious choice to slow down to seed time or rock time, to sill the clamoring ego, to set aside plans and busyness, and simply to be present in my body, to offer myself up." How can we offer ourselves up to the subtle rhythmic sway and flow of Nature? Can this really be done in a society in which overworked or stressed-out individuals perform all their duties without once ever planting foot on terra firma from the time they leave their home to the time they return? Perhaps the secret is in taking small steps toward creating opportunities for stillness and contemplation. Just a few minutes here and there—to breathe more deeply, to think more slowly, to perceive Nature around us with greater awareness, or perhaps to perceive the world within our soul.

What if we begin by placing a single chair or bench outside

so that it faces a small flower bed in our yard, a special tree, or even a seasonal planter? I met a young man recently who, in absence of a garden, has tendered a small potted plant on his bedroom windowsill for three years. With warmth in his eyes, he shared with me that *this* was his Sanctuary Garden. He sat before the plant in a few minutes of silence each day, quietly noticing a new leaf node here or a flower bud there. There is a lesson here—to give ourselves permission to sit as often as possible before a bit of Nature without judging ourselves as to the time duration—to offer our attention unconditionally. Season by season, we can observe the same scene, letting it teach us through its subtle shifting.

When I was a new mother, my partner and I left the city, taking our two-month-old son and moving to a wild piece of property on the Olympic Peninsula in Washington. Miles from civilization, we lived contentedly in a tiny cabin with a dirt floor. On the crudely built deck that literally hung over the edge of a steep little valley, I placed a single planter box, fashioned from an old wooden crate. Because our garden space was to be carved out of a deep thicket of alders, and much water had to be hauled by hand to water it, I contented myself in the early stages with this one-planter garden full of bright annual flowers. I sat for hours, nursing my son, gazing across the valley, and admiring my flower box and its daily growth. It was one of the happiest periods of my life, where I was utterly content to be still, reflecting on the miraculous new life in my arms, in the beauty of Nature around me, and in my synthesis of human and Nature, as reflected perfectly in my simple little flower box.

CHAPTER 22

"Mother in the Garden"

by Sarah Gorham

In the morning the light tilts
over the roof
and splits into a hundred parts,

each shift glowing around a vegetable.
Behind me, I can hear the seedpods
drop from the locusts

and spread themselves over the lawn.
One here, one balanced at the edge
of the garden. With their darker color

they are unmistakable
and adjusting my arms to each
location, I rake them in.

A few cotton socks and the wood pins
flip over the clothesline.
I shut my eyes

and the children begin to rustle,
some of them calling from every corner
of the house. They'll have breakfast:

a special spoon, a plastic saucer
under every bowl.
They scoot their little trucks

across the floor like shoes
until all I can see is a row of shoes:
each one unfastened, expensive.

A patch of grackles swoops down
as I approach. Now
I can hear my husband, pausing

before he steps outside. It's ten o'clock
and he's mumbling about the weather.
I offer him anything he can imagine.

CHAPTER 23

"Oral History"

by Debra Landwehr Engle

It is a Thursday afternoon in December, just over four months since my mom's most recent heart attack. The enormous sycamore leaves from her front yard have been windswept into the beds up against the house, and the locust beans that cover the ground like a plague of black in the fall have been raked and left on the curb for the composting trucks. Yesterday my mom spent the day pain-free; today she's weak and having some angina. She is lying in bed listening to "Talk of the Nation" on the radio when I let myself in the front door. I'm not sure if she's awake, so I peek into her bedroom and wait until she opens her eyes before I say "Hello."

Like my brothers and sisters, I come to her house often to check in on her, and because I enjoy sitting in the living room where I grew up, watching television with her or catching up on small talk. Today, though, we are about to span three centuries of time. She is going to take me back to her childhood, all the way back to the home of her grandmother, who probably gardened years before my mother's birth, in 1915, clear back into the nineteenth century.

I never knew my mom's mother, let alone her grandmother. The generations passed and skipped before I was born, and old photographs tell me little. I never smelled these women's cologne, never fell asleep to the cadence of their voices, never heard their skirts swish as they went down the front-porch steps. I am about to learn more about them than I have ever known, all because of gardening. Gardening leads to baking, which leads to a creek and a quilt and a pump organ and my aunt's boyfriend and quail pie. It all comes from the garden. Everything comes from the garden.

"People didn't have nurseries back then," my mom says of her grandmother's era, "and they were better gardeners." In the early 1900s, her grandparents lived near Myrtle, Missouri, just above the Arkansas line. Their house sat on Doniphan Road.

With her fingers, my mom draws the layout of her grandparents' property on the coffee table. "The house was *here*, and the apple orchard was back *here*," she says. "Granddad planted every kind of apple there was. And the barn was back here. The garden was large, between the orchard and the barn."

She remembers it well because she and her older sister Grada spent many days there. The girls' own home was separated from the Fairview schoolhouse by a creek. When the water rose in the spring and became impassable, my mom and Grada lived at their grandparents' house, which was on the same side of the creek as the school. Despite the felled tree that served as a bridge, my mom fell in the creek once. "They had to wrap me up and put me in front of the fire," she says.

A lilac bush hid one corner of my great-grandmother's porch; a prolific vine climbed a trellis at the other end. "She had beautiful roses," my mom says. But most striking of all were the plants beyond my great-grandmother's garden: the wild roses growing along the fence across the road, right in front of an entire field of wild daisies. "Grandpa wasn't fond of those daisies," my mom says. After all, they usurped perfectly good pasture ground. For my mom, that field of daisies taught an early and simple lesson: In a world of constant work, sometimes wonder trumps utility.

In her childhood, the lines between work and play blurred as she gathered gooseberries for pie or ate black haws from wild bushes on the way to school, or climbed down into the cellar, using the trapdoor in her grandparents' living room floor, to gather apples and sweet potatoes.

She and Grada sat on the front porch for hours at a time, peeling apples and peaches from the orchard. Their grandmother then spread out the slices on a bedsheet and left them to dry on the roof before she and her daughter turned them into a twelve-layer cake. "Sumptuous," my mom says. It is one of many things that she declares as "the best thing I ever ate."

So there it is. A picture. A verbal photograph. My great-grandmother was a lilac bush, a peach tree, a safe harbor from a swollen creek, a view of daisies dancing in the sun.

When I turned forty-eight last October, my mom gave me a stoneware pitcher that she remembers from her childhood. Inside it, she tucked a handwritten note that says, "This belonged to your Grandma Hall. Your grandma knew how to bring a room to life with an apple blossom branch, forsythia, or pussy willows. I remember this vase being used often for this purpose." I brought home the vase and filled it with two branches cut from our burning bushes. They lit up the kitchen table for several days before the crimson leaves started to fall.

My grandmother was magic with roses, my mom says. She could take a cutting from a rose, put it in water, turn a fruit jar over it, and set it in the sun, and it would grow. "I've tried it two or three times and never had any luck," my mom says.

Like her grandparents, my mom's parents gardened not just for beauty, but to live. A garden was sustenance, insurance that no one would starve through the winter.

My mom remembers watching Bernie, the hired hand, walking behind a mule and a plow as her father cleared fields of trees, and how the plow would get hung up on the tree roots, and Bernie and the mule would keep going. She remembers how rich that soil was, a storehouse of energy from hundreds of years of decayed leaves. She remembers how she and Grada made hats out of saucer-sized sycamore leaves, pinning them together with thorns. She remembers that, while her father cleared land, she built miniature cemeteries, using rocks for tombstones and gathering flowers to lay on the pretend graves; this, she says, might have been a tribute to her twin brother, who died when they were almost three.

She remembers walking to Myrtle once to buy a quarter's worth of sugar, which she estimates now at about two and a half pounds. She had to cross the creek on a swinging bridge, which was fun one minute and scary the next. Her mother bought coffee and peanut butter. And she bought flour to make the breakfast biscuits she served with fried squirrel. She made dumplings, too, and quail pie. Again, my mom says, "It was the best thing I ever ate."

My mom's memories of her mother and grandmother are connected, because her experience of them was simultaneous. That's why I'm surprised when she tells me she doesn't know where her mother grew up. "Mama talked about what a beautiful spot it was," she says. "It sounded like the Garden of Eden. I'd give anything to know where it was. I think it was over the line in Arkansas."

Then she tells me a story about her cousins, relatives whose names I've heard but can't picture in the family tree. It seems that a relative named Rufus signed a paper pledging not to get married until his father died. Rufus kept his word, taking care of his ailing father, and postponing his own marriage. When his father passed on, Rufus moved with his bride to the family farm, which he inherited in exchange for his commitment.

The real point of the story is that the bride had a son, a young man named George who dated Grada for a time. When my mom, at the age of eighteen, took a job in Jefferson City, Missouri, she ran into George and started a relationship of her own. "That always pleased me," she says, "because Grada stole some of my boyfriends."

Ah. So my mom still has the spirit of a young girl. Maybe it's because her mother was a branch of apple blossom, a cutting from a rose, a bit of lingering mystery.

* * *

A few years ago, for another birthday, my mom gave me the latest quilt she had finished. It's a Flower Garden quilt, a design of small hexagons, some cut from prints, some from solid muslin. My mom started it as a teenager and finished it six children and six decades later. She edged it with a narrow red binding, a metaphor for the brick border around her flower beds.

Her flowers ringed our backyard, growing even in a bed south of the house where only our next-door neighbors could see them. Because of my mom, I lived my childhood in proximity to flowers. They were always in the background, even when my mom bundled them up and set them in a vase with their arms outstretched and their heads held high and they filled the house with fragrance. I was not a gardener, my mom did not teach me to garden. But they were there, a backdrop of tulips and poppies for my childhood.

My mom did not intrude. She did not give advice. She did not teach me to shave my legs or talk to boys or apply lipstick. She did teach me to sew and to make meringue cookies with chocolate chips and nuts and to stir cornbread into a glass of milk the way she had in the Ozarks as a child. But she did not teach me to love flowers. Like her mother and grandmother, she just loved them herself.

On my mom's coffee table are computer printouts showing antique pump organs. Her cousin in Arkansas has the organ that my mom and Grada played when they were little. My mom hasn't seen the instrument since about 1930; she didn't know it was still in the family. One of the printed photographs reminds her of her grandmother's organ, with Victorian scrollwork and shelves for bric-a-brac. My mom remembers playing this one, probably on those days when there was no way to cross the creek and she and Grada lived with their grandparents, smelling the lilac bush by the front porch and admiring the field of daisies across the road.

My mom's cousin doesn't have room for the organ anymore and wonders if someone in our family would like to have it. Thinking about the organ has made my mom remember her grandmother's garden. And recalling her grandmother's garden has made me think about this thing called generation and legacy.

I am trying to sort out nostalgia from longing, as if there were any difference. I think of rocks that became headstones and sycamore leaves that became hats and berries eaten on the way to school, sometimes falling to the ground and squishing up between bare toes like the dust in the road. I'm thinking about a time when life decisions were dictated by a swollen creek, and you had everything you needed to survive growing within a few dozen yards of your house.

I am thinking about the ways we come to know one another. I will never hear the exact words of my great-grandmother or grandmother, although they speak through the generations in the language of flowers. But I can get a glimpse of them, and the glimpse becomes a picture, just as every river or apple tree or gooseberry bush is part of the earth and *is* the earth, all at the same time.

I have been taught that, if you turn your inner and outer world into a garden, people will come and sit with you there. I come often to sit with my mother. Today, I have learned something important. I have learned that my mother, like the women before her, is the scent of peaches drying on a roof, the energy of a rose sprouting in the sun, the perennial flowers that form borders and backgrounds in quilts and backyards. From generation to generation, mothers and daughters pass a link to the earth. An omnipresence, always rotating, always giving life.

CREDITS AND PERMISSIONS

from *Around the House and in the Garden* by Dominique Browning. Copyright © 2002 by Dominique Browning

"Stardust Tomatoes in the Kitchen Window" copyright © 2005 by Doreen G. Howard

"Gardening with Louise" copyright © 2005 by Judith B. Tankard

"Mother's Day Visit" by Briggs Nisbet. Copyright © 2005 by Briggs Nisbet

Excerpt from *Cultivating Delight: A Natural History of My Garden*, pp. 26–27, by Diane Ackerman. Copyright © 2001 by Diane Ackerman. Reprinted by permission of HarperCollins Publishers Inc.

Excerpt from "The Garden in Winter" from *My Garden (Book)* by Jamaica Kincaid. Copyright © by Jamaica Kincaid. Reprinted by permission of Farrar, Straus and Giroux, LLC.

"Seeds for My Mother" copyright © 2005 by Linda M. Frank.

"My Grandmother's Aprons" copyright © 2005 by Patricia Lanza

"A Time of Renewal" by Nancy Hutchens reprinted with permission of Pocket Books, an imprint of Simon & Schuster Adult Publishing Group, from *A Garden's Grace* by Nancy Hutchens. Copyright © 1997 by Nancy Hutchens

"The Need for Solitude, Stillness, and Reflection" by Christopher Forrest McDowell and Tricia Clark-McDowell reprinted with permission of Simon & Schuster Adult Publishing Group from *The Sanctuary Garden* by Christopher Forrest McDowell and Tricia Clark-McDowell. Copyright © 1998 by C. Forrest McDowell and Tricia Clark-McDowell

"Mother in the Garden" by Sarah Gorham first appeared in *Ploughshares* (Spring 1979) and was later reprinted in *Don't Go Back to Sleep* (Galileo Press, 1989). Copyright © by Sarah Gorham

"Oral History" copyright © 2005 by Debra Landwehr Engle

About the Authors

Diane Ackerman's works include *An Alchemy of Mind*, *Cultivating Delight*, *A Natural History of Love*, and the bestseller *A Natural History of the Senses*. Ms. Ackerman has received many prizes and awards, including a Guggenheim Fellowship, the John Burroughs Nature Award, and the Lavan Poetry Prize.

Cathy Wilkinson Barash is president of the Garden Writers Association, a lifelong organic gardener, a prize-winning internationally published food and garden writer and photographer, the author of eleven books, an edible-flower maven, and a nationally recognized speaker.

Dominique Browning is the editor in chief of *House & Garden*. She lives in New York City with her two teenage sons.

Frances Hodgson Burnett was the author of *Little Lord Fauntleroy*, *The Secret Garden*, and *Sara Crewe* (later rewritten to become *A Little Princess*). She died in 1924.

Debra Landwehr Engle is the author of *Grace from the Garden: Changing the World One Garden at a Time*. Her articles and essays have appeared in *Country Home*, *Country Gardens*, *Better Homes and Gardens*, and other national publications. She and her husband live in Madison County, Iowa.

Linda M. Frank is a writer, organic gardener, and dried-flower designer. Residing in New Jersey with her husband and cat, she chronicles tales of human and garden nature.

Sarah Gorham is the author of three collections of poetry: *The Cure*, *The Tension Zone*, and *Don't Go Back to Sleep*. Recent poems and essays have appeared in *Poetry*, *American Poetry Review*, *Virginia Quarterly Review*, *Gettysburg Review*, *Prairie Schooner*, and *Poets & Writers*. Gorham serves as president and editor in chief of Sarabande Books, an independent literary press, which she cofounded in 1994.

Louise Hallberg runs the Hallberg Butterfly Gardens in Sebastopol, California, a butterfly-friendly nonprofit garden.

Penelope Hobhouse is a garden writer, garden designer, garden historian, lecturer, and gardener. For fourteen years, until 1993, with her husband, Professor John Malins, she was in charge of the National Trust Gardens at Tintinhull House in Somerset, England. Today she lives in Dorset and travels in Europe, Australia, and the United States, lecturing and designing gardens.

Doreen G. Howard is editor of *Easy-Care Landscaping*, a contributing editor at *Mother Earth News*, the former garden editor at *Woman's Day*, and a regular contributor to numerous magazines. She gardens and lives on a glacier moraine at the Illinois-Wisconsin border with her husband, Peter, and dog, Brandy.

Nancy Hutchens is the author of *Memories of a Midwestern Farm* and *A Garden's Grace*. She lives with her husband in Westchester County, New York, and works as a management consultant when she isn't gardening.

Jamaica Kincaid is the author of numerous books, including novels; *Talk Stories*, a compilation of her *New Yorker* writings; and an anthology of writing on plants. She lives in Vermont with her husband and children, and she teaches at Harvard University.

Barbara Kingsolver's ten published books include, among others, *The Poisonwood Bible*, *Animal Dreams*, *The Bean Trees*, and *High Tide in Tucson*. In 2000, she was awarded the National Humanities Medal, our country's highest honor for service through the arts.

Charlotte Matheny Kirkwood was an early Oregon pioneer and the author of *Into the Eye of the Setting Sun*. She died in 1926.

Patricia Lanza is a book author, freelance writer, and lecturer. She lives in Florida and Michigan with her companion, Dave Wood, and a host of stuffed animals who come to life in their children's books. She is the author of *Lasagna Gardening*, *Lasagna Gardening for Small Spaces*, and *Lasagna Gardening with Herbs*.

Maud Lindsay was the founder of the first free kindergarten in Alabama. Her first book, *Mother Stories*, was published in 1900 and was quickly followed by *More Mother Stories*. Maud Lindsay's writing of children's stories continued until her death in 1941.

Sharon Lovejoy is an award-winning nature and garden writer and illustrator. She is a contributing editor for *Country Living*